THE PHONE RANG

How Three Sisters Navigate
the Destructive Path of Leukemia

BookVenture Publishing LLC
1000 Country Lane Ste 300
Ishpeming MI 49849
www.bookventure.com
Hotline: 1(877) 276-9751
Fax: 1(877) 864-1686

Ordering Information:
Quantity sales. Special discounts are available on quantity purchases by corporations, associations, and others. For details, contact the publisher at the address above.

Printed in the United States of America

Library of Congress Control Number: 2015935130
ISBN-13:   Softcover   978-1-942703-65-5
                  hardcover   978-1-942703-66-2
                  Pdf   978-1-942703-67-9
                  ePub   978-1-942703-68-6
                  Kindle   978-1-942703-69-3

Rev. date: 06/09/2015

Disclaimer
This publication is designed to provide accurate and personal experience information in regard to the subject matter covered. It is sold with the understanding that the author, contributors, publisher are not engaged in rendering counseling or other professional services. If counseling advice or other expert assistance is required, the services of a competent professional person should be sought out.

THE PHONE RANG

How Three Sisters Navigate
the Destructive Path of Leukemia

Dr. Mary Reid Gaudio

Contents

Dedication

I dedicate this book to my son Richard Jacobs, his wife Marla, and children, Evan and Juliet—you keep me focused on what's important in life; and my husband, Gino Gaudio, who makes life worth living. I am so grateful for all the doctors and organizations that saved Ann's life. In order to continue their great work, a portion of the proceeds from sales of *The Phone Rang* will go to Roswell Park Cancer Institute and Hope Lodge in Buffalo, NY and weSPARK in Sherman Oaks, CA.

Foreword

This is the true story of three sisters (Ann, Mary and Chee) finding out that Leukemia does suddenly run in our family. This is our process, how we dealt with it, what issues came up and how we all survived. Hopefully, our voices will help you understand what it's like for a family to go through this horrendous ordeal and how we took each step to overcome our fears and insecurities. We were clueless about how to proceed but we found our way together. From Roswell Park Cancer Institute in Buffalo, NY, to Hope Lodge in Buffalo, NY to City of Hope in Los Angeles, CA and weSPARK in Sherman Oaks, CA we have a lot to be thankful for.

Survival Mode

"Give me a head with hair, long, beautiful hair, shining, gleaming, streaming, flaxen, waxen. Give me it down to there, shoulder length or longer, here baby, there momma, everywhere daddy, daddy, HAIR, flow it, show it, long as God can grow my hair. Let it fly in the breeze and get it caught in the trees, give a home to the fleas in my hair." Yes, Ann was in the musical HAIR in Italy. Flinging her hair around and singing her heart out, standing there naked surrounded by the American flag. Ironically, she lost her hair at least twice during her bout with leukemia and a few months later she lost it again due to her bone marrow transplant. Ann's hair is back now. It's dark and curly, not like her previous hair. She thinks it's because of her donor. She thinks he must have short, curly, dark hair. Everyone's leukemia is different. This is our sister Ann's survival story, from the point of view of me and our younger sister Chee. Our brother, Paul, is also a part of this story but he doesn't say too much. You'll be hearing about him here and there. We're all about five years apart so our memories of each other are very different. Chee hardly remembers Ann at all as a child. I think she said no memories! Ann went away to college when she was 17 years old (SUNY Fredonia for two years then Boston University after she married her childhood sweetheart. Our parents belonged to a Mr. & Mrs. Club and Ann and Richard played together as children when our parents would have Christmas parties and picnics. Her husband, Richard Collin, got a Danforth and Woodrow Wilson scholarship to Harvard University and off to Boston they went.) So Chee was about two years old. I was seven and Paul was twelve. Ann's concept was that she was an only child for 5 years so when Paul came along she thought, "What do you need him for? You've got me??" Can you imagine how she felt when Chee and I entered the world?

Cut to fifty years later. Ok, so Chee called and said, "Ann is not feeling well. She says she has the flu and it won't go away. She called the doctor and the doctor said to come in for some tests." Chee decided she was going to drive her in immediately because she was too busy during the week. Ann was complaining about how cold she was and that she couldn't warm up. Ann always took good care of herself. She saw the best doctors and always scheduled appointments during her breaks to take care of her aches and pains. I'm not sure if she knows this, but she was known as "Agony Annie" to some as a little girl. Our mom told us. We always tease her that some of her illnesses were possibly due to Paul being born, then me, then Chee! What did our parents need us for? They had Ann! Wasn't Ann enough for them? Ironically, for the last five years she was not crying wolf or needing attention. This was the real thing.

Chee's version: Saturday, February 25, 2012

Since returning to Buffalo from Los Angeles in January, Ann had not been feeling well. (We thought she may have been traumatized. She had her gold jewelry stolen off her neck when she was walking in Long Beach with her long time friend, Jack Gallagher. This young thug jumped in front of her and yanked the gold off her neck in broad daylight. The kid took off down the street with no one to do anything about it. This incident was very disarming.) Anyway, Ann had been going to the doctor regularly and they were not able to pinpoint the problem (thought maybe MERSA, shingles . . . .) She was going every morning to get antibiotic shots. The doctor decided to do a more elaborate blood test. Ann received a call from her doctor, Dr. Nashiha Shahid, at about 8:15 AM on Saturday morning instructing her to go to Strong Memorial Emergency Room in Rochester because her platelet count was low. She took several blood tests to be sure and saw a high white blood cell count. (The doctor received a call, at home, from the lab people on that Saturday morning, so it must have been very important.) Ann called me and said the doctor wants her to go to the emergency room because of the low platelet count (of course, neither one of us knew what that meant). Ann told me she just wanted to go home and go to bed. I told her, "You have to go today because I'm too busy next week and you know you won't feel any better." I said I'd take her right away, but I called the doctor back to see if we could go to Mercy Hospital in Buffalo because all of her records were there, or if she really wanted us to go to Strong. The doctor told Ann no problem going to Mercy, and I could stop by her husband's office (he's a pediatric doctor) and pick up a copy of the lab results-Ann's doctor would have the lab fax them to him. I went to the doctor's office and spent about a half hour there while they were tracking down the report. Ann said we didn't have to leave right away, but I wanted to get her there before their day got too busy. We left about 9:30 AM; it was typical blistery winter weather in Buffalo, NY.

10:30 AM—We checked into the emergency room at Mercy Hospital. It wasn't too busy yet so there was no waiting around. They immediately did blood work. The initial blood work came back and the emergency room doctor said the way her counts read it's often leukemia. Ann and I both laughed and said "Oh no, our family doesn't get leukemia!" Many, many, other tests were done. Ann had fallen flat on her face on some ice at the farm the week before and had a big bruise. They did a CT scan of her head and saw no problems there. They did a scan of her lungs to rule out problems there, and they picked up a problem with her spleen. They did a better CT scan of her spleen and it looked like there was a laceration so they were talking about a possible spleenectomy. Another doctor thought perhaps mononucleosis. We asked doctors about the low platelet count. They said a normal count is 100,000+. The test her doctor did was at about 19,000. (Platelets make your blood clot—with it this low if she injured herself she could bleed to death.) By the time she was at Mercy it was hovering around

10,000. I had mentioned to one of the doctors how I wanted to get her in before it got too busy with the Friday night hangover crowd. The doctor laughed and said they call it the "brunch crunch" when people start showing up about 11:00 AM and continue increasing throughout the day. By early afternoon the place was overflowing. Paramedics were in the hallways with people on carts, etc. I didn't know this but the nurses explained that when an ambulance/paramedic/EMT bring someone in they cannot be relieved until the patient sees a doctor. That's why there's so many people milling around.

Phone Rang: 9:00 AM

Mary: Ann had told me that she wasn't feeling well the last time I talked to her on the phone. She said she had low energy. Chee told me that she was going to take Ann to the doctor so they could do some tests. I knew that Chee's schedule was pretty tight during the upcoming week so it had to happen this weekend. The doctor said to take her immediately so there was no waiting, even though Ann thought it could wait. The next phone call I got—at 9:00 AM, Chee told me or rather this is what I heard "They said her blood count is really low. It's supposed to be 1000 or 50,000 or something like that and it's at 9. It doesn't make sense. I have no clue what they're talking about yet. They said she could have leukemia . . ." or blah, blah, blah. Brain tuned out. Wait. What?

We laughed. She couldn't have leukemia. It must be a mistake. That's not in our family. Our family doesn't get sick. We dismiss this idea. We chit chat a little longer. How's the weather there? Is there a lot of snow? Any skiing? Any snow at the farm? Wish we could go snowshoeing, etc. We had so much fun the year before when I was at the farm at Christmas snowshoeing around our property and checking out all the animal tracks. We snowshoed around the Big Pond then down to the Little Pond and across the field to the apple orchard. This is where the deer like to hang out. It was cold and blizzardy. Sometimes it's like Siberia there in the winter. But it's incredible when you go inside to warm up and have hot chocolate and sit by the fire, or when we make pizza in the pizza oven at the Big Pond under the picnic shelter. Ann had a friend from Italy build a pizza oven next to the picnic shelter and one year we made Christmas pizza. Delicious!

My then fiancé and now husband Gino Gaudio and I were in the car on our way to someplace as Chee and I were chatting. He was listening to our conversation. I shared with him the doctors' speculation and I totally discounted it. "That's just crazy. That's not our family."

Next phone call, I think it's the same day— "They're checking her into the hospital to do more tests. I'll call you when I know more."

Wait. What???? I don't understand. What kind of tests??? I'm stunned. (Head spinning and all that stuff). I shut down and watch stupid TV. It's like the kids playing video games till all hours of the night to veg. My son, Rick, used to play video games after football practice in high school and also in college—UCLA. He probably still does after a hard day at work in court. He's a lawyer now. I like The Housewives of New York and The Housewives of Beverly Hills. I also love Andy Cohen's Watch What Happens, especially when he has guests put on wigs and read contentious scripts from the Housewives shows. I saw Liam Neeson and Joan Rivers do this. It was a tribute to Joan after she died. Boy do I miss her making me laugh on Friday nights with Fashion Police. Hilarious! The Rich Kids of Beverly Hills is fascinating, too. They make me laugh out loud. They really are very funny, especially Morgan. I love both cities, NY and LA, and it is sooo much fun to see where everyone's hanging out—the restaurants, Central Park in NY, Malibu in LA and of course Beverly Hills. Both cities are another character in the show. I lived in NYC before I headed to Aspen, Colorado to become a ski instructor. I didn't have time for television then at all! My friend from 7th grade, Lori, went to grad school at Adelphi University and when I graduated from SUNY Fredonia she convinced me to move there so I shared an apartment with her in Garden City, Long Island. We had a great time going to bars with my guitar and convincing the bartender that I should sing there. I played cover songs that people requested and I mixed it up with my original songs. Lori knew all my original songs and would be so frustrated with me when I messed up the lyrics. Sometimes I switched verses or made up new lyrics. She would sing along and didn't like it when I changed things around. Sorry Lor! I also lived on E. 50th for a short time until I bailed and moved to Aspen with my first boyfriend, Gary. Gary and our friend, Patrick Hasburgh (he wrote 21 Jump Street, Hardcastle and McCormick, Aspen Pulp the book and Aspen Extreme the movie) moved to Aspen first and became ski instructors. In Aspen Extreme, Peter Berg played my boyfriend, Gary, and Patrick told me the blond radio DJ was me. In real life, Gary was a drinker, not a cokaholic. You have to see the movie to understand what I'm talking about. As east coast ski instructors, we would video tape each other when we were on the Glenwood Acres and Kissing Bridge Ski School and we read Ski Magazine voraciously. We could envision ourselves flying off huge cliffs in the Rocky Mountains and landing in powder a mile deep. Anyway, Gary came back to NY to get me and we drove back to Aspen in his camper. There was a garbage strike in NYC that year so I was ready to split. I remember it took forever to cross flat, miserable Nebraska. We kept looking for the Rocky Mountains, nowhere in sight. We drove to Aspen in Gary's camper (slept six) which had seen all of Vermont ski areas. We'd ski all day, make dinner and eat in the camper, drive to the next area, go to sleep and wake up with the dawn patrol and ski all day there. We skied Cannon Mountain, New Hampshire, Stowe, Vermont, Mad River Glen, Mount Snow . . . That's the only way you get good at anything—obsession. Since we chewed up and spit out the east coast we ventured out to the west coast. We had a blast in Aspen that year. Partied with Fleetwood Mac and met all kinds of celebrities. I didn't stay as long as Gary and Pat did though. At the end of the ski season in Aspen, we decided to drive the rest of the way across the country and see the Pacific Ocean so we drove to Los Angeles via Park City, Utah, Snow Bird, Alta, Squaw Valley, CA and San Francisco (yuck, rainy and too much like Buffalo). We skied everywhere and drove down the coast toward Los Angeles. When I landed in LA, I loved it and stayed. Gary went back to Aspen. I worked as a temporary secretary at KCOP where I met my first husband, Barry, and had my son, Rick. No longer a ski bum! Well kind of. I actually taught skiing at Mountain High and Bear Mountain in Big Bear for many years. It's hard to shake the habit! Rick learned how to ski when he was 2 years old. I held on to him between my legs and took him down black diamond runs just as he was learning to walk. Fearless!

Chee's thoughts: After many, many tests were done there was no conclusion. They did talk on the phone to the surgeon who did her colon surgery a few years earlier (what an episode that was) and sent him spleen test results. He said he didn't think the spleen was a problem. They concluded they wanted Ann to spend the night and have the specialists have a go at her on Sunday (particularly a blood doctor). They found a room for her about 6:00 PM; I stayed until she got settled in and left around 7:00 PM. I asked the doctors if they were going to do anything about her low platelet count, why we originally came in. They said no. I chuckled, she had gone from getting daily antibiotic shots and who knows what else she was taking, to nothing. I figured they wanted her blood clean so they could ascertain the problem. Boy, was I right!

Sunday: The Phone Rang—8:00 AM

Mary: The next phone call from Chee came a day later, "Ann has leukemia. If I didn't take her in to the doctor when I did she could have been dead in a couple days. It's a fast growing cancer. She's going to start treatment right away."

What kind of treatment? Am I dreaming? Is this a nightmare? This is crazy. They must be making a mistake. They must be reading the test results incorrectly. I'll get another phone call from Chee soon telling me it's something else. They discovered a blah blah blah in her "I don't know what" and a minor surgery will take care of it all. She'll be back in commission in no time. Just another little scare in the life of Ann Reid! We're used to this by now. She always had a flare for the dramatic. As a little girl, I remember her making her "entrance" when she would walk into a room. Sometimes it was elegant and sometimes she would be like Lucille Ball and do a prat fall. I used to watch her put her pin curls in her hair before going to bed. I was four or five years old and she was in high school, fourteen or fifteen. She was so beautiful and interesting to me, very funny, too. She went to Immaculata Academy Catholic School for girls in Hamburg, NY. Luckily, I didn't have to go to a girl's Catholic school. Dodged that bullet! I played violin and the public school in our neighborhood offered a great music program and advanced academics so I negotiated with our parents that I would continue playing violin if I didn't have to go to Immaculata! I really wanted to quit violin because all my friends were quitting playing their instruments but Mom and Dad outsmarted me and wouldn't let me. I hated violin. So they let me take up guitar, then flute and then viola. I was also taking piano lessons at the time. Very clever of them! Chee and I both benefited from this. She played viola, was in advanced classes and even graduated a year early! Paul had to go to St. Francis Catholic School for boys on Lake Erie. I remember the dinner discussions about his grades. He would have dessert taken away when his grades weren't up to par, but he didn't care so that didn't work very well for anyone. I don't remember any of his consequences. Paul had to go through a few tough things as a little kid. He had an issue with his eye and had eye surgery when he was about a year old. Dr. Lewin was his eye doctor so of course we named a pet after him. Our little white bird was called Dr. Lewin. Snowball, the cat, would salivate over the bird and one day we came home from church and the bird was gone, eaten by Snowball. It sounds like a cartoon, doesn't it? The next incident, Paul was jumping off the picnic table with our cousins Big Paul and Karen and he broke his leg. I think he was around three or four. So Paul had to wear glasses and a cast on his leg before he was five years old!

Cousin Karen, Ann, Mom and Paul at Steuernagel's well. That's our
house behind them. Chee and I weren't even a glimmer yet.

Paul was a fantastic big brother for me. He taught me how to play
all sports—football, basketball and baseball and I'd have to be on the
teams in the neighborhood because there weren't enough boys. I loved
it. He was very patient with me and I excelled. Later I became captain
of the girls' basketball team in middle school called the Xerxes and we
were undefeated. Paul used to babysit Chee and me and he let us stay
up and watch The Twilight Zone. I had horrible nightmares from it
and to this day I will myself not to dream. I know William Shatner on
the wing of the plane was one of the episodes that scared me to death.
One time Chee fell asleep and she was sleepwalking into the kitchen.
She squatted down and started picking at the floor. We laughed so hard

because when we asked what she was doing she told us she was picking strawberries. Then she got up and went back to bed. Another major event in our childhood was when Chee gave her Chatty Cathy a bath and Chatty Cathy stopped talking. Not a sound. We prepared a funeral and Paul gave the string one last pull. She talked! She was saved! What a relief! During the winter when school was cancelled, we made fifteen foot snowmen, dug fort tunnels along the side of the road and made fox-chase-the-goose trails all over the neighborhood.

Now Ann was a different story. Immaculata was great for Ann. The nuns loved her because she had such a beautiful voice—like Maria in The Sound of Music. They wanted Ann to become a nun. She sang like an angel. She was in all of the musicals, which of course I attended. But one thing I just couldn't understand was that she would always miss the bus in the morning and I didn't get it. Why? I couldn't wait to go to school! How could she miss the bus??? Our mom would have to put me and Chee in the car and tote us to school and back. I vowed that I would never miss the bus when I went to school! (I just intentionally overslept because I was skiing on the weekend and didn't write my English paper. So I wrote the paper and hitched a ride to school in time for PE and study hall.)

Back to being five years old, on weekends or after dinner, I would listen to Ann play the piano and I wanted to take lessons so badly. Paul was playing, too. Things like Chopin's Little Doggie Chasing his Tail, The Volga Boatman . . . I had to wait till I was five. That's what Mrs. Warren said. She gave all the neighborhood kids lessons.

Paul, Ann, me and Jerry Birk, a neighbor friend.

Oh yeah, I also remember Ann saving me in the pond at the farm. I dashed into the pond thinking I could swim (I was about six years old) and I looked up at Ann from about a foot under the surface of the water. I actually remember this vividly. She just reached down and yanked me out of the water. I was quite scared after that. It took me a while to get back in the pond. It's amazing, all these memories flying by my eyes and brain in split seconds. Then there was the hornet's nest incident. I was jumping off some logs in the back yard at our home in Blasdell. I'm seeing a pattern here. Our family likes to jump off things apparently. Dad was gardening nearby. He always kept the farm in Cattaraugus and our home gardens in Blasdell pristine. Mom was at a Girl Scout meeting I think. I was happily jumping away off some stacked planks of wood in the back yard when hornets swarmed around me stinging me everywhere. I screamed at the top of my lungs! I remember Dad swooping in like Super Man and pulling me out of the center of the angry hornets. He ran me to the kitchen and Ann put a mixture of baking soda and water paste all over me which took the sting out. I was afraid to come out of the house! I remember slinking along the side of our house, hugging the wall. Ann and Dad encouraged me to re-enter the world and eventually all was forgotten, at least for the moment.

Ann got married to Richard Collin when she was nineteen at Our Mother of Good Council Church in Blasdell, NY. That means I was nine and Chee was four. We were her flower girls and we had little white dresses and baskets with flowers in them. Ann wore a short white silk dress and a little veil over her face. There was a garden reception in our backyard for all the friends and family and our yard looked so beautiful. Dad had the lawn looking impeccable and the picnic shelter was all spruced up. Beautiful linens were arranged on the tables. It looked like a Martha Stewart outdoor bridal party. Our mom was a Home Economics major at Buffalo State College and she made all kinds of canapés and sweets for months ahead of time. Our dad was a perfect match for our mom. He built the house that we grew up in and our mom decorated it for her final school project. Oh, Ann's wedding was just beautiful. All our friends, family and neighbors joined us at the garden party at our house. The immediate family was invited to a breakfast reception at The Old Orchard in East Aurora near Orchard Park—home of the Buffalo Bill's Rich Stadium. Our parents had their wedding reception there and their 50th wedding anniversary. All major events in our family were always celebrated at The Old Orchard.

Our grandfather, Paul Scholl, owned The People's Dairy in Blasdell, NY just south of Orchard Park and East Aurora. He was in competition with Rich's Dairy. Mr. Rich married Paul Scholl's sister-in-law and our great aunt, Victoria Payne. But her carriage was hit by a train in Cattaraugus, N.Y. and Aunt Victoria was disabled. Her sisters, one being my grandmother, took care of her after the accident because Mr. Rich divorced her. That was the end of that. No one talked about it much at all. There was no association with the Rich family. No one seemed to know anything when we asked questions. People who would know anything aren't alive anymore.

When I was 15 years old, I skied regularly at Glenwood Acres/Kissing Bridge Ski Area just south of Buffalo. I was president of the ski club at my high school so I had lots of ski friends. We actually skied as a family and I started when I was around 5 years old. I don't remember skiing with Ann but she also skied.

Ann skiing at Chestnut Ridge Park.

We went to Chestnut Ridge Park and the Buffalo Evening News had a free ski school. Paul, Chee, Mom, Dad and I would go once a week. Then as I got older, Dad took me and my friend Maryjean Steuernagel (now Kraengel) on Thursday nights for the Courier Express free ski school at Glenwood Acres. I eventually became a ski instructor at 16 years old. This is how I met Gary and Patrick and we became ski bums together. I sang and played guitar at the Red Barn, an after-ski restaurant, and one afternoon Ralph Wilson, owner of the Buffalo Bills who played in Rich Stadium stopped in for a drink (see the connection? The man who married my Aunt Victoria, Mr. Rich, and left her after she got hit by a train? We actually were related to the Rich family by marriage). Some ski instructors plunked me up on the juke box and I played a couple songs for Mr. Wilson. He gave me twenty dollars and that was the beginning of my singing career! I sang in NYC, Philadelphia, Aspen, Colorado and Los Angeles, CA.

Eventually, Paul and I put together a rock band called Che Blammo and KROQ and KLOS played our music—Stupid for Your Love, Antiseptic Love and many other stupid love songs. We played at Madame Wong's East and West, Club Lingerie, The Central (now the Viper Room owned by Johnny Depp) and many other clubs in LA. Our rhythm section worked with Eric Burdon from The Animals— Terry Wilson and Tony Braunagel. We also worked with Katie Sagal's keyboard player. She played Peg Bundy in the television series Married With Children. Wow, my brain is just swirling with scenarios of my life, my sister's life, my family's life. It's interesting how near death experiences, even of family members, make you analyze your life.

Gurf Morlix on lead guitar, Tony Braunagel on drums, me on rhythm guitar, Terry Wilson on bass and Paul on keyboards at Madam Wong's in Los Angeles.

Gurf, me, Tony, Terry and Paul rehearsing in Los Angeles.

Back to Chee: "Chemotherapy I guess. The leukemia is called ALL—
Acute Lymphocytic Leukemia. Google it. It's very aggressive. It's
most common in children and treatments result in a high chance of
recovery. It is very rare in adults though and the chance of recovery
is greatly reduced."

Mary: What the hell are you talking about? This doesn't happen to
us. Our dad did get brain cancer but that was a fluke. He worked in
construction as a plaster mason so we think he was exposed to chemicals
in the air, such as asbestos, or something. He was the healthiest human
being I ever knew, mentally and physically. I don't even know what to
think or how to act. This is very confusing. Do I go home to be with
her? What can I do? It seems like we just went through this with Ann
when her colon burst and I spent the whole summer running back and
forth from the farm to the hospital fifty miles away when she was in an
induced coma. I wonder if the two are related? Leukemia is a disease
that attacks the immune system and Ann's immune system had been
severely compromised with infections that wouldn't heal. When Ann
was in the coma, she told us she was traveling around the world on a
great but strange adventure and when she came to, she was in a field
of yellow flowers. I was standing next to her in a yellow scrub gown
holding bright yellow sunflowers. Funny girl!

Chee: Sunday, February 26, 2012

Ann's all safe and snuggly at Mercy Hospital. I called her but did
not go in. She said they were going to do more tests, etc. She called
me about 4:00 PM to say the doctors have concluded she had ALL,
Acute Lymphocytic Leukemia. If Ann had not come in when she
did she very well could have been dead in a couple weeks! They
said we're going to transfer her to Roswell Park. We both agreed
nothing was going to happen on Sunday, doctors won't be around
. . . . . Boy, was I wrong again!

Maryjean Kraengel (she's a close friend of the family and also a
nurse) called me about 7:00 PM (I'm not sure if I called Maryjean

or if Ann did). She told me Ann was transported to Roswell already. There was no waiting till Monday! I called Ann and she said yes, she's there, and she's already been seen by her team of doctors led by Dr. Elizabeth Griffiths, and they have diagnosed ALL is Acute Lymphoblastic Leukemia (also called Acute Lymphocytic Leukemia). They will be starting treatment immediately!

Mary: I can't believe what I'm hearing. I'm three thousand miles away and feeling very helpless. Ann's not a child so does she have a lower survival rate? Will she survive? We just spent Christmas together and had a great time. Her friend Jack Gallagher came out to LA and we had holiday dinners and parties with friends and family. She was fine! When she left for NY she was starting to get a cold but I thought she just wasn't slowing down and taking care of herself. Having too much fun! I figured Ann kept teaching her classes and would go home exhausted. Or maybe she was stressed over her gold necklace being ripped off her neck in broad daylight when she was walking with Jack in Long Beach. A friend had given it to her over 30 years ago. Very frustrating! What can I do? How can I help? Illness in a family affects everyone. We were all concerned, scared, frustrated and you couldn't picture what was going on when you're so many miles away. You couldn't read anyone's face or look in the doctor's eyes to see how serious it really was, or how scared Ann really was. She was so exhausted that I think she was just happy to be in the hospital and people were taking care of her. I don't think she was really aware of what was going on around her although it wasn't as bad as the last hospital experience. She was in an induced coma then and every day a different major organ would fail. We didn't know if she would come out of the coma ok or even live through this ordeal. She didn't even know how upset and concerned we were with her son Oliver because he was afraid to get on a plane to see her. I don't know how Paul felt but I was really pissed and so was Chee. Oliver had all legal rights and he was three thousand miles away. No medical decisions could be made without his consent. The only thing we knew was that the doctors kept saying her son needs to be there. Nothing bothered Ann. She was sleeping!

On top of all of this chaos with Ann, our mother, Maribell, was in the final stages of her life and we were all trying to take turns to be with her at the same time trying to process what was going on with Ann. Our brother, Paul, was at the farm full time making sure our mom didn't hop in the car and drive away. Paul said she's in the "terrible nineties" stage of her life rather than the "terrible twos". When you asked her to get up she'd say "No." When you'd say, "You have to eat, Mom" she'd say, "NO!" Anyway, Mom was 93 when Ann first got leukemia and mom really didn't understand that it was her daughter that was so sick. Mom was always saying that she wanted to go home but we couldn't figure out which home she meant. The one where she grew up in Cattaraugus on Waverly Street? The home in Blasdell on Burke Parkway that our dad built? Or the home where she lived as a teenager with her brothers at People's Dairy? This is the dairy our grandfather started in Blasdell, NY that was in competition with Rich's Dairy in Buffalo. Our mom used to drive the milk truck from our farm in Cattaraugus to the dairy in Blasdell. She ended up living in Blasdell and went to school there for her senior year. This is when she met our dad, Richard Joseph Reid—football and basketball star. Dad joined the Coast Guard after high school and mom went to Buffalo State College. They got engaged and mom couldn't wear the engagement ring on her hand when she attended college. It was against the rules. So she wore it as a necklace around her neck. This was the 1930s. Interesting. Dad landed in Pearl Harbor just after it was bombed during World War II and had to clean up. Paul, Chee and I wouldn't be here if he landed there earlier. The Coast Guard wanted our dad to become an officer but he just wanted to go home and be with our mom. Sweet. He built the house we grew up in and our mom and dad filled it with love and security. So charming.

Before all this, Ann made a lot of the appointments for our mom. Our mom had developed an unusual condition—a prolapsed uterus—and the pessary that was holding up her uterus had grown into her body. Years earlier, she decided not to have a hysterectomy and preferred the use of the pessary instead. The problem was none of us knew about it. She had been involved with a national study called the Women's Health

Initiative for 10 years, from the time she was 75 years old till she was 85 and the doctors were checking her regularly. At least we thought so. Like I said, she was about 93 years old at this time. Her doctors had never seen anything like it. She desperately needed surgery. Ann was making the phone calls and fighting with the insurance people who kept saying they weren't going to pay for it, because of Mom's age. Ann was getting experience with the health care system by helping our mother and now she's fighting for her own survival. What strange tricks are played on us! On the day of our mother's surgery, after months going back and forth with the insurance company and finally getting approval for the surgery, we were told that the insurance company decided not to pay for the surgery. Now what! We called our friend Maryjean, the nurse. We called the hospital where the surgery was going to take place. The doctor told us to bring her anyway and we did. The insurance company did pay finally. Our mom's surgery and condition is now in the medical books.

A Elinor, The Oratorio

Mary: A year before Ann got sick with leukemia she decided to stage a new production of AElinor, The Oratorio about Eleanor of Aquitaine. Of course I would be there, so I went to Batavia, NY and Ann's college, to participate in her production of AElinor. Since we would all be in town, Chee decided to have a celebration for her son Joseph because he finally finished his Eagle Scout requirements. Chee and her husband Mike had been arguing and negotiating with Joe for years to get him to complete it. This was the event where Gino and I reconnected after not seeing each other for ten years. Ann knew Gino and his previous wife when she was in Pirates of Penzance and we would all see each other at parties Ann had when the tour ended. Gino and I would also run into each other when we worked at Universal Studios.

Vinnie Adams, Arnold
Schwarzenegger and Mary
at the opening of Conan the
Destroyer.

Richard Brose and Mary in the
Conan the Barbarian poster

I was in the live action Conan the Barbarian Sword and Sorcery
Spectacular and Gino was in the live action A-Team Show. He and his
wife would buy Peugeot cars from my brother Paul. I didn't even know
about this until Gino told me when we re-met!

Gratci and Rick in the MG

I have a photo of my son Rick and Gino's daughter Gratci (four years old) sitting in my MG when they came to visit and buy a car I guess. We can't remember any other reason why they would be there! This must have been in 1985. Eventually I got divorced (1989) and later Gino got divorced (1994). We hadn't been in contact at all for years because I was immersed in my doctorate program at UCLA and working on promoting my career in education. Ann invited Gino to sing in her production at her college in Batavia, Genesee Community College. She picked Gino up at the airport and brought him to the Eagle Scout ceremony the day before the production and our eyes lit up when we saw each other. "You haven't changed a bit, except for a few grey hairs!" I said and we hugged. That was it for now. Chee asked me to speak at Joe's ceremony and I prepared a few inspiring words. I think I shared my favorite Buddhist prayer:

May I be at peace,

May my heart remain open,

May I know the beauty of my own true nature.

May I be healed,

May I be the source of healing in the world.

My other job for this event was to get Mom up and dressed for Joe's celebration. Mom and I were staying in Ann's home in Batavia and I went in to the bedroom to get her up and she refused. I begged, "Mom, please get up. We have to go soon. They gave me the job to get you ready!" and she stated, "They gave you the hardest job!" That was that. She wouldn't get up. I went back about 10 minutes later and she finally behaved. We put her beautiful black mink coat on her and she looked very regal. I was so proud of Joe. We all were. His brother James, who already finished his Eagle Scout requirements, participated in the ceremony, too. It was very inspirational. James is working on his acting career now in LA. Joe has been accepted into University at Buffalo and will complete his Bachelor's Degree.

Ann wrote a grant for the AElinor production which she now calls an Oratorio. She hired an orchestra and a choir with the money. Her young students played Henry and AElinor and they were outstanding. A little crisis occurred just before the AElinor production. I was supposed to play viola in the orchestra but the narrator got sick and Ann asked me to narrate. After a little convincing, I said yes. I was prepared for playing the viola, not narrating! That's a different mindset. But I pulled my acting chops out of my sleeves and had a great time. Crisis averted. Roberto Bonani (he was in the Italian production of Hair with Ann in Italy) also flew in with Gino and sang in AElinor. Roberto played the Pope. Gino and Roberto are good friends and they met through Ann, too, about thirty years ago. Gino wanted to study Italian (he speaks fluently now) and Ann thought Roberto would be perfect. We had a blast performing together. Ann used to invite us to perform in her shows for the Lehman Engel Musical theater workshops in Los Angeles and this brought back such great memories. But the icing on the cake for me was Gino! We had our first ever kiss in Ann's kitchen after the show. Roberto made his famous pasta and after dinner I took a handful of dishes into the kitchen and Gino followed me. I couldn't run away, which I usually do when I'm in an uncomfortable position, and the kiss was so nice I actually leaned in. Wow! Amazing! We talked for hours afterward. Who knew we'd fall in love?

First Hospital Stay

Mary: Ann was admitted to Roswell Park Cancer Institute, famous in Buffalo, New York and all around the world for finding cures for cancer. As an interesting aside, Chee went to grad school with Roswell Park IV who is the director of the Academic Support Programs at Buffalo State College. His great grandfather was Roswell Park. Ann said she was exhausted and so happy to be taken care of by so many efficient doctors and nurses. She couldn't figure out why she was so cold and her flu symptoms would not go away. She said she went to work and would go home and get into bed as soon as she climbed the stairs. She was constantly fatigued. At least we have some answers, even though they're shocking answers. I talked to her everyday and I knew Ann was relieved that she was in good hands.

Ann closed her eyes and sailed away to her days on tour with Carol Lawrence (married to Robert Goulet) in Funny Girl. Her life flashed before her eyes as she talked to me about her adventures. Ann was a voice major at Boston University and the stage was calling her, apparently. As a little girl I loved her exciting life. I wanted to be like her when I grew up.

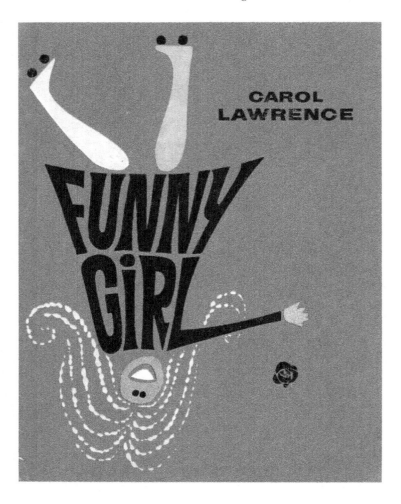

Ann told me in her dream state, "This was my first equity show. I was singing with the Washington and Arlington Operas, so I had my AGMA card. I did smaller roles, things like Suzuki in Madame Butterfly. I learned a couple roles, such as Giovanna in Rigoletto and Mimi in La Boheme. I could sing art songs or arias from operas as audition pieces. I worked with Metropolitan Opera singers at the time and the National Orchestra. I was also singing at the Roma Restaurant in Washington, D.C. One of the customers came up to me and said that there was a regional audition for Broadway shows and you should go to it. He told me where it was and I

*went to the audition in Washington and from that initial audition I was
invited to go to NY and audition again for specific shows. I didn't know
anything about it but Richard (husband) and Oliver (son) all got in the
car and went to NYC. Oliver and Richard went off to a local park and I
went to the call back. I was a member of AGMA, the performing arts guild
for opera, ballet dancers, people like that. These auditions were pretty small,
maximum 40-50 people. So I get there and the line is around the building!
There are over 600 people, girls only, because this is a women's call back.
I was just stunned. I'd never seen anything like this in my life! And they
were all call backs! And we found out they were casting numerous shows. I
forget the exact number. There were tents all over the east coast. They would
produce the show and you'd be there 2-3 weeks and then off to the next tent.
So they were casting for around 10 shows, maybe more. There was one in
Buffalo called Melody Fair. They used it as a rock venue for a while but then
they tore it down I believe. I didn't have to dance. In those days, there were
dancers and there were singers. Not like today. I must have been around
22 years old. I got married when I was 19 and had Oliver when I was 20.
I sang something from the lyrical musical theater. There wasn't much pop
music like there is now. I was singing nightly at the Roma Restaurant so my
voice was in shape and I was pretty hot! I probably sang something from My
Fair Lady or Oklahoma. This was in the 1960s so these were current shows
at the time. I passed everything and they told me I got the job, right then!
There was a lady from our Union, Equity, at the table and they signed you
to a contract and at that time you were scheduled for your costume fitting
for the next week. I took the train. Richard was in the army at the time,
working at the Pentagon. We had a modest salary. You didn't make a lot of
money in the army. We rented a little house in Arlington, VA and our car
was from Henry Steuernagel, our neighbor from Blasdell, NY. He sold us
a Pontiac for $75.00. Daddy approved because it was in good condition.
We used the car for 2 years when Richard was working on his doctorate in
archeology at Harvard after receiving a Danforth and Woodrow Wilson
scholarship. He got very uninterested in archeology but timing is everything
and Richard was called to active duty by the U.S. Army. I finished my
Bachelor of Music at Boston University. Then Richard was sent to boot
camp with all these friends that we made. He applied to the Pentagon and
was sent there. He was in officer training in Harvard (ROTC) and he was*

an officer by this time, I think a Captain. They were all officers actually and they were all sent to Viet Nam, except Richard. We lost touch with them completely. Richard was trained in intelligence and reconnaissance work and spent two years in the Pentagon on the staff of the Assistant Chief of Staff for Intelligence. At this time he was an analyst and briefing officer for Middle Eastern and North African affairs."

"I started studying with Wilkie, Frederick Wilkerson, at least two lessons per week. He taught people from the NYC opera and he was a good friend of Roberta Flack. That's how I knew Roberta.

Frederick Wilkerson at his piano.

Wilkie's studio would be invited to certain events and one of them was President Johnson's boat on the Potomac River. It was a Texas Barbeque for military men, veterans, etc. So we were invited to perform for veterans. That's when Roberta played the piano for me. She can play anything in any key and she has a photographic memory. She's an outstanding person and musician. At that time she was a music teacher in the Washington public schools. She played every night in a bar in Georgetown. This is where she developed her fan base. She would sing and play. Later on one of the directors I was working for said he loved this song by Roberta Flack, "Killing me Softly". I said I knew Roberta Flack. You do, he said. Yes, we both studied with the same teacher in Washington, D.C. I called Wilkie and he was the one who "ordered" her to come to Italy to do the film I was in. Yes, and I wrote the words for the song, she sang two songs. One was a love song and in those days there were usually two songs in a film. That would be in the 70s. One is the song for the credits and the other is the love song during the scene. One song was called, "It Wasn't True" because the film was actually about a man falling in love with a prostitute. He was in love but was worried that it wasn't true, this love that they had, because she could go away at any time and he could be just another john. He couldn't trust her. The first song was "Let Me Be". We recorded in a little studio in Rome with a group of the best musicians, my friends. Antonio studied guitar with Segovia in Spain. He could play anything in any style. A composer I worked for named Danilo Partucci was the bass player."

Ann is the tallest show girl standing in the back row, Carol Lawrence was the star, Teresa Merritt played the maid and Sylvia Syms was Funny Girl's mother. Dancers in the front row first on the left are Mary Jane Houdina and the second person on the right is Michon Peacock.

"Ok, back to Funny Girl. Carol Lawrence's children were on tour with her and I had Oliver with me. So they played together. She was lovely to me. Robert Goulet, her husband, would visit her frequently in the various cities we would play in, when he was free. We were all over the east coast. We wouldn't go to big cities like NY and Chicago. We would go to venues in Long Island and Connecticut, but that was for the entire summer. I became very friendly with a group of people from the show. One person was the stage manager, Larry Smith, and he and Richard became friendly. Richard did tour with me frequently because he was waiting for his assignment. Larry had a girlfriend, Michon Peacock, who was a dancer in the show. She later helped write the musical "A Chorus Line". The characters in the show were a composite of real dancers. Another girl from my show, Mary Jane Houdina, became a Broadway choreographer. These were my good friends that I hung out with. I was always frugal and I didn't want to spend my money on bars *and restaurants. I saved the per diem. I was invited to go on for another three month contract but Richard got the assignment to go to Italy so we decided to go on another adventure. I must have been 22 and Oliver must have been two and we were off to Italy in September. Richard had gone on ahead, I think in August, because I remember I was alone with Oliver. The army came and packed up our stuff, including our car. I didn't have to do anything. Then Oliver and I got on the Pan American plane, I remember the girls in the blue uniforms, and we went off to Europe. A few weeks later our stuff arrived! Oh hi Chee, what are you doing here?"*

Chee: Monday, February 27

I went to Roswell to see her, and brought all kinds of stuff from her house, mainly her computer, music system, etc. Her room was nice, overlooking Lake Erie and the wind turbines. Similar view to what she had at Mercy when she had her colon incident. (Ann had a colonoscopy two years earlier and it burst. Peritonitis set in and she almost died then but that's another story.) Ann was at Roswell for about 4 weeks—that's how long the first round of chemo takes. They did discover her hernia surgery wound was infected so they took care of (or so they thought) that problem. She was released around the end of March. It was decided she would go to the farm to recuperate since people were there—Mom, Mom's caregivers, Paul, the county nurse, etc. Lois, the county nurse added Ann on as a client. At least twice Ann went to the emergency room in Olean due to fever. After a few weeks at the farm, she was re-admitted to Roswell. Then the new adventure begins.

The Phone Rang: 11:00 PM — Second Hospital Stay

Mary: Ann returned to the hospital for a second time. Apparently, the treatment wasn't working. She had an ongoing infection and they didn't know why. The doctors started pumping her with antibiotics and trying to fit in all the chemo treatments. I was on the phone with her daily and so was Chee. The infection was sabotaging the chemo and they had to stop for a bit while they dealt with one thing at a time. At first they thought the gauze used to close up the incision after the colon fiasco was causing the infection. The doctors were trying every combination of antibiotic that they could imagine. As I understand it, they finally discovered that staples used to close up her incision from her previous near death experience was causing the infection. The staples were removed and the infection was finally under control. I think this is when Maryjean (Steuernagel) Kraengel went to the hospital to check on Ann and she thought Ann may not make it. The chemo was taking a toll on her body and the infection was throwing every organ out of whack. We were all rightfully scared.

Chee's version, March 2012

Ann was scheduled for another round of chemo. I brought her computer, music equipment . . . . . . back to Roswell. It was ascertained the staples in her hernia wound were deeply infected.

The staples were removed and all kinds of specialists were brought in to figure out what kind of antibiotics she should be on. The wound had to be cleaned and repacked every day. Antibiotics were given intravenously. She was at Roswell for about another month. Once the chemo round was done and the infection somewhat under control, she was released to a rehab facility—she still needed the daily intravenous antibiotics and cleaning of her wound. She was at the rehab facility for a third month. We brought her car there and she could leave for the day but couldn't be gone overnight.

The Phone Rang: 8:30 AM

Chee: Saturday, April 28

I was driving Mikey Kate (daughter) to a Feis (Irish Dance Competition) in Syracuse and I got a phone call from Mom's caregiver Theresa at 8:30 AM stating that Mom was having chest pains and was being taken to the hospital. I got back from Syracuse at 3:00 PM, dropped Mikey off at a friend's house for the night, and stopped at home to get overnight gear. I'm not sure if I would be taking Mom back to Cattaraugus, or booking her into the hospital and coming back to Batavia. I got to Mercy about 4:30 PM. Theresa was at the hospital, Mom was fine and wanted to go home. Oh no, you're here and the doctors want to run more tests. Conclusion: she was fine so I drove her back to Cattaraugus about 7:30 PM. It was concluded that one of Mom's caregivers over reacted to Mom's situation. When Mom would get like this we'd calm her down, give her a couple aspirins or Tylenol, and usually after an hour she would be fine.

Mary: It's a competition when the phone rings. Is mom sick? Is Ann ok? Even worse, did one of them die? I got the phone call that our dad died early in the morning November 13, 1989. That's when it happens you know. My stomach sinks when the phone rings at 6:00 AM. Whew! Good news! We found out that Ann qualifies for a bone marrow transplant which can save her life. But this can't happen until they're sure all of the leukemia is out of her body. How does a bone marrow transplant work? So many questions! How does the bone marrow work? We found out that the siblings have to be tested. Oh ok. Paul is over 60 years old so he won't have to go through the process. Chee and I have our blood tested, Chee in Buffalo and me in Los Angeles. What an ordeal that was for me, trying to find a lab that would do it! Then we learned that neither Chee nor I was a perfect match. I was very disappointed. So . . . . on to the donor bank. They found a perfect match in a young man around 23 years old and we were ecstatic! A few days later, he decided he didn't want to do it and our hopes were shattered. They kept trying. God, will this horrible rollercoaster ride ever end! Ann was happily being taken care of by the wonderful nurses and doctors at Roswell Park Cancer Institute. They had such a passion for their work and they were so kind to Ann. They obviously wanted her to live or they wouldn't put so much time and energy into trying to figure out all the problems she keeps encountering! This whole process would cost a couple million dollars if she didn't have good insurance. Or they wouldn't do it at all. Or if she was one year older they wouldn't have done the Bone Marrow Transplant (BMT). What a horrible thought that is!

Life in Rome Italy

Another hallucination was coming on. Ann closed her eyes. Fatigue set in. Now she told me she was in Washington, DC with her husband Richard. He was working at the Pentagon. They got the news that Richard was transferred to Rome, Italy and off they went with three year old Oliver. Rome was sunny, warm and full of possibilities. Ann worked with stars in Spaghetti Westerns, met and befriended a Countess and was in the Italian version of Hair. Richard was overt CIA or DIA (Defense Intelligence Agency) and read all the newspapers to try and figure out what the Italians were really thinking.

She traveled on in her dream world and continued sharing her visions with me. "Hmmmm . . . Let's continue", she said. "Well, my first impression of Rome . . . . my husband had taken over the house in Rome that his predecessor had lived in, it was a villa. We had a lovely garden with lots of olive trees.

Ann in her back yard with the olive trees in Via Deiva Marina, Rome.

I was so impressed by these olive trees. I just loved olives and as a little girl I would steal the olives off people's plates at dinner parties! Our furniture had not arrived yet. Waiting . . . I did my best to make our villa look beautiful when our furniture finally arrived. The villa was very Italian, you know, the gorgeous tiles, open al fresco patios and lots of bougainvillea. Richard was not a state department employee in Rome. He was employed by the Defense Intelligence Agency in 1967—DIA not CIA—although it was affiliated and had offices in the American Embassy. Evidently every country in the world has a DIA. For five years he served as Chief of the Intelligence Collection Branch of the DIA station.

His job was to make reports on things. For example, the Russians were displaying their aircraft, farm machinery and things like that in Italy and Richard was required to go to these showings and I would go with him occasionally. They were interesting. It was overt intelligence and that meant that you would go to a local fair and report on it. You would read the papers and report on what you would read in the papers. It's not covert where you sneak around underground and try and get into people's groups. They can't keep you out of the fair because he's American. He would look at things, we'd buy things. People didn't ask why we were there. We had some very good friends who were medical students and somehow some of their friends at the university learned about Richard and thought he was CIA and beat him up. The Italians are leftists along with the Parliament and the Christian Democrats, Socialists and Communists. So you have a real disparity. It's probably more of a democratic society than ours where we only have two parties. Anybody who can get the votes can be seated in Parliament. You have some crazy parties. One of them was led by a very famous stripper. So you had those factions of the country who did not like Americans. During this time when we were there, there were the Red Brigades which blew up the train station in Milano at the end of August when everyone in Europe goes on vacation. That was a communist group. Our friends remained friends. The university students beat up Richard and they did not do their research, thinking he was CIA and possibly trying to get information from Lorenzo. They were part of our life in Italy. We went to a lot of places with them."

"I went to the Conservatorio di Santa Cecilia after about a year of living in Rome. I was bored sitting in my villa! I studied music. I was there taking the course work but never pursued getting the degree. I met a friend at the university who introduced me to my agent, Jack Repp. He was an American. I had a great photographer who made me look beautiful. The photos were just gorgeous! Even in the theater you don't get made up like that. Your hair and makeup is very general. But for the cinema, especially the Italian cinema, everything is so precise. The major part of the work I did in cinema was costume drama. I'd never be an Italian woman. I'd always be English or a Swedish girl. I was surprised I didn't look like an American to them, I looked Swedish."

"There was an open audition for the musical Hair at the Teatro Sistina in 1970. Of course I went, and I was hired! Renato Zero, Loredana Berte and Edoardo Nevola became big stars after this show. I was in the show for a year. We did quite a few weeks of rehearsals where we learned how to be a group of

hippies. Roberto Bonanni played the famous Claude. Teo Teocoli and Carlo De Mejo played Berger. The English director was Victor Spinetti, the translator was Giuseppe Patroni Griffi and the producer was Franco Cancellieri. Bill Conti, who composed the music for Rocky, became the musical director for HAIR when Bill Elliot left the show. Penny Brown was the protégé of an important Italian star of the theater. He had wanted Penny to be the star in Hair. When I auditioned they said I would be part of the tribu but I said no, I had to have a song or something to make it worthwhile. So they gave me the song "Good Morning Star Shine" to sing and they divided the lead part of Sheila up between me and Penny! We became great friends. I enjoyed that very much.

Penny Brown, Bill Conti and Ann Collin (Reid) in Milano, Italy.

About half way through the show, I got a herniated disc from carrying Ronnie on stage on a stick upside down. Penny and I had to carry him and he was pretty heavy! We were in Milan and I had to go to the hospital for a couple weeks. Richard had to get me in the station wagon and our friend Lorenzo DiMedici, who was studying to become a doctor, came over to the house and gave me shots of B12 which helped me feel better."

"Back to Hair! Because we were in Rome, we had to pay respect to the Vatican. They were going to censure the nude scene. Our director and the producer fought to have the nude scene because it's integral to the story, freedom, love and the whole message of Hair. So they agreed to turn off all the lights. We could do the nude scene but it would be in the dark. The press got wind of this and on opening night they flashed their cameras and it was absolutely all lit up! Everyone was standing there nude! It was funny and terrifying!!! No one expected it! There were over 100 cameras from every journal and international paper you could think of! After that no flash cameras were allowed. But the producers of Hair did something very lovely. It was the Sistine Theater and they projected on the walls and ceilings famous nude paintings and sculptures, such as David, Venus, etc. and we're standing on stage and we're naked with all of these world famous and ancient and modern nudes surrounding us. It was very beautiful and artistic. I was in the show about 2-3 months when Richard announced that he would like to try the nude scene with us. So we said ok here's what you're going to do. You're going to be back stage and during the nude scene you'll come out and Penny will be on one side and I'll be on the other. The big American flag will come down the aisle and it's silk and flowing and we're singing . . . We'll all go under the flag and we'll take off all our clothes and then we'll stand up naked. So Penny went backstage and got Richard and it was dark and he was under the flag with us. We're all taking off our clothes and it's the moment to stand up and Richard forgot to take off his t-shirt! He had on his American undershirt which was stark white so in the light this big undershirt is all you can see. The production people didn't notice so he grabbed his clothes and ran off. We've been laughing about that for years."

Mary: Sorry for the interruption. Around now our mom and dad decided to take Paul, Chee and me to Italy and visit Ann. This was in the early 70s just before I went off to college. Ann was trying to get me to stay in Rome and study music there, viola specifically. Dad said no, he wasn't going to lose another daughter to Italy. Richard drove us around in their VW van and Oliver translated for us. He was only seven years old. We went to The Coliseum, The Spanish Steps, the Trevi Fountain . . . We stayed in a pensione and went shopping in Florence. I bought leather items: leather pants and shoes. We went swimming in the Mediterranean Sea and I had my first experience with a pervert. I was in the bathroom and someone was pushing on the stall door. I said, in English, "I'm in here!" When I opened the door and walked out he grabbed me and I slugged him really hard and ran. I didn't tell anyone until we were in the van speeding away. We had long dinners at night. We'd go to dinner at 7:00 pm and not return home until 11:00 PM or midnight. It was actually fun sitting around talking to each other and hearing my parents' point of view in a different environment. Chee and I were underage and we remember how much fun it was having wine with dinner. I remember the family walking together in the evening and some guys were saying something really disgusting in Italian. I only knew because Ann was yelling at them that this was her father and she screamed, "Don't talk like this in front of him!" It was all in Italian but you could figure it out. I had just graduated from high school with five years of New York State Regents Exams in French under my belt. You know—the romance languages are similar. Ann, Chee and I were tall blondes—five feet ten inches. We must have driven the boys crazy!

Chee, Ann and Mary in Ann's back yard in Via Deiva Marina, Italy.

Ann, Richard and Oliver in Italy.

Ann continued, "I worked for The Dino De Laurentis Studios. I worked there for months and months in a film called Waterloo with Orson Wells, who played Napoleon. Rod Steiger and Christopher Plummer also starred in it. The director was a famous Russian named Sergei Bondarchuk. I played an English woman and I was Wellington's mistress. We spent months rehearsing this dance which took place at Wellington's mansion. De Laurentis's daughter was in it and she was supposed to cry. We were all worried and stood around trying to help her. Eventually she did cry."

Ann in Fregene, Italy. This is one of Richard's favorite photos.

"Another film I did was with Jack Palance called Si Puofare Amigo. This was shot in Almaria, Spain. In English it's called Can Be Done. I actually wrote the song for the film. It's a series of films and they're funny western or spaghetti westerns. I was his lead girl. That's where I met Dany Saval who gave me the heart necklace that I wore for 30 years. It was ripped off my neck in Long Beach that day. She was the lead actress in the movie but she was a big Disney star. She was married to Maurice Jarre, a French *film composer of the films Dr. Zhivago (Laura's Theme) and Lawrence of Arabia. They had a daughter together. I actually stayed with her in Paris in her beautiful apartment. They had a personal chef who made the most magnificent food! For some reason she was mad at him and would say, "Should I fire him?" I didn't know the reason. I thought whatever he does this food is so great it didn't matter. One story, at that time it was illegal to take money from the US to France. So she sold a couple condos, property she had in the US and bought a big diamond. She stuffed it somewhere and marched straight into France. She knew someone who would give her the appropriate millions that it was worth, $20 million or so. Anyway, we'd go back and forth from the studio. I was there at least a month. The film was shot up in the mountains which you would swear was the American West. It looked more like the west than the west looks today. We stayed in a hotel in the town and every day we had to go up to the mountains where the set was located. I had to ride with Jack Palance frequently. He was very disdainful of me. In the film, I played a prostitute and we wandered back and forth across the west in this wagon. Jack Palance was the guy who put together this group of prostitutes. He was the boss. Maybe he was staying in character. Once he said to me, "So what else do you do?" I thought maybe he thought I really was a prostitute. I said, "Well you know I have a degree in music from Boston University." "You do?" he said. "My daughter wants to get a degree in music." I said, "I highly recommend it. I also write songs." "Oh you do?" he said. After that he was much gentler with me. He hardly spoke ever, ever, to anybody. He was really gruff and did not want to be bothered. The experience was very nice. His real name was not Jack Palance. His brother was Jack. His brother was his agent in Rome. I met his brother numerous times in Rome through my agent, Jack Repp. I also remember that the other star in the movie, Bud Spenser, was Italian with an American name. Italians do not trust food from other countries at all. He had his people, his cook, drive a whole caravan from Italy to Spain to bring his spaghetti. It had to be Italian food."*

*Ann is in bed with Jack Palance in the movie "It Can Be Done, Amigo"
directed by Maurizio Lucidi.*

Ann and Jack Palance negotiating where they should go next.

Ann is the Madame with her girls and Bud Spencer.

Ann and Bud Spencer were discussing the girl's fee. Maybe not . . .

"On another film, I remember they would send a limo to pick me up at about 5:00 am and the limo would drive way up in the mountains. We shot in this old, old church. I mean, it was from medieval times. It had beautiful paintings on the wall. It was very sparse. Italians go crazy for costumes. They had costumes from the period of Italian opera which went from the 1600s right straight through till the present. There are four centuries of costumes stored in these warehouses. So they have the exact costume for the period including the exact underwear. So of course, you're all corseted up. This was the 1600s and we had to wear metal cylinders. Think of paintings of that period where women had their breasts squashed. It goes all the way down and it laced in back like a corset. Everything is strapped down, and of course I fainted by noon! You just couldn't breathe in the damn thing. This went on for maybe five or six days and the limo would come and get me and take me home at midnight. There was no union organizing the hours you could work. They take you home at midnight and pick you up at 5:00 am the next morning. The makeup and costume takes all day and then you go down to the set to shoot for five minutes."

"I did a film with Lando Buzzanca. He was like a Jay Leno comedian. I played the Swedish girl where I come into his apartment (I invented this whole thing) and I had a fur coat which I threw over my shoulder and then dragged on the floor. As I entered his apartment, there was this huge kiss. My name was Ulla and I was hired by the director. I was told by him that I would play Ulla. I was sitting in the dressing room and another agent brought in some of his girls and I heard him tell her that she was going to play Ulla. I went to the director and I said, "Am I supposed to be Ulla?" He said, "Yes, of course." I said, "Well, they're preparing another girl in the dressing room to play the part." "What???" he said. He went to the dressing room and straightened them out. I couldn't believe I had the balls to do that!"

Here is Ann as Ulla the Swedish girl with Lando Buzzanca.

Lando Buzzanca with Ann having a good laugh.

"Eventually I started writing lyrics for film music. I was in a film produced by an Egyptian producer, Anis Nohra. He lived near me on Via Nuova Aurelia. He lived in an apartment building less than a mile from our house. We would go back and forth in the limo every day. And again he asked me, "What else do you do?" And I said, "Well, I have a degree in music." "You do?" he said. "Do you write songs?" I said, "Yes of course!" I never wrote a song in my life! He said, "My wife writes songs for an Italian publishing company and she wants to get out of song writing to write scripts. She's tired of writing songs." I said, "Well I'll write songs." He said, "Fine I'll have her call you." So I was very grateful. Sure enough in a few days I get a call from Audrey Nohra . . . And she asked me if I would come in to the studio to write songs. They sent me a CD of the orchestra completely done. I had to come up with words for songs completely finished. I was a lyricist. They needed me because I could write the lyrics in English. They had plenty of Italian lyricists. Songs were distributed all over the world in English. Sometimes the director would call me and talk to me and sometimes I worked with the composer. When I tried to become a composer for film music in the US, I discovered that the composer and the director have some sort of relationship. They went to school together or they know each other through friends, something like that. So the composers, none of them were women. The wives will not let you anywhere near them. There are a lot of important women in filmmaking now but they work under the composer. They'll frequently write the music and do the orchestrations but he'll put his name on it. He's the one that has the relationship with the director. So I would frequently work with the composer who was buddy buddy with the director. Danielle Pattuchi is one composer. I worked with all the major Italian composers except the one that always works with Fellini, Nino Rota. I never worked for him. He had staff."

"This must be around 1976. I was touring with Tony Cuchiara, and he was a big pop star. He was writing these musicals. It was mostly a setting with songs. So I did a couple shows with him and he had grants from the Minister of Shows—Ministaro dello Spectaculo. It was a Cabinet position where somebody controls the shows that are going on in the country. They do this in Italy. It's like the NEA—National Endowment for the Arts. We toured these little tiny towns, especially in Southern Italy. They were considered less culturally advantaged then those in the north. It would have been in the 20s during the time of

Mussolini, that there were 200 theaters in Italy, maybe more, that did opera. That means there was an orchestra, soloists, chorus, dancers, etc. There were only twenty theaters in 1976. These tiny little towns had these old opera houses that were virtually kaput. But the theater was still there. So it was our task to open these theaters and use them again with these musicals. So we had interesting little experiences. In one town, we opened the theater and all the pigs were housed there. We had to spend the whole afternoon before the show cleaning off the stage. Another little theater in another little town, when we got there in the last earthquake the dressing rooms had fallen off the theater and down the cliff. So there was a big hole in the back of the theater! You could look down the cliff and see the dressing rooms down at the bottom!!! So we all had to get dressed in public, in front of all the other cast members. You had to find a little niche where you could put your costume on. I always played the American girl and one of my songs was "Sono L' America" – I am America. It was immigrant America so I had little boots a long skirt and it was a period piece of the late 1800s when many Italians came to the US."

"During this time I worked with Meme Perlini in Avante Guarde theater. The Mickery Theatre in Amsterdam is where we did Othello. It's the version written in the 1100s and the author is Cinzia. Later Shakespeare wrote his version in the 1500s. It was similar but the characters were more political. For example, Cassio was a big fat naked man and he was also portrayed by a pig in a cage and we did this at the Biennali di Venezia and we were invited to go to Paris. We did the same show in L'espace Cardin which is Pierre Cardin's theater on the Champs Elysee. We were there a couple of months, we played a month and then we were there rehearsing. By the end of the run, did that pig stink! I wonder if they ever got the smell out of the theater. In the L'espace Cardin the pig was big and horrible and it would snort during the performance. It would upstage everyone and Cassio would come out and the lights would go on the pig, then the big naked man, then the pig . . . . Our performance of Othello at the Biennele di Venezia got Newsweek Magazine award as one of the 5 best shows of the year in the world. That was the late 70s. Those were interesting experiences. I worked with Meme Perlini a couple of years and also with Tony Cucchiara. The movies were only one or two days. The only movie that filmed a long time was at the Dino DeLorentis studios where I was Lady Hamilton, Lord

Nelson's mistress—the Duke who won over Napoleon at Waterloo. We were there a month. The shooting was maybe a week."

"In Tarzan, I play a British lady with my parasol and I'm supposedly viewing my garden. That's where the picture of me with the burning umbrella is from. There was no garden there but I'm standing in front of the armoire and this hand comes out and lights my umbrella on fire. It was a stunning scene, this big black armoire, what was in there? Some sort of monster? This was the type of avant garde theater that Meme Perlini enjoyed creating. No rhyme or reason. Just visual scenes unrelated to Tarzan. You'll have to ask Mr. Perlini why!

Ann in Tarzan: There is an armoire behind Ann. She is holding an umbrella. An arm comes out of the darkness from the armoire with a lighted match and sets the umbrella on fire.

Tarzan was a group of scenes like this. There was an undertone of darkness in all the scenes. At one point, Meme Perlinni came out and peed in a bucket. He peed to the front of the audience but you didn't see his penis. He was wearing like a floaty shirt and pants. We got invited all over Europe— France, Holland, Italy."

"Lisy De'Scalzie was the Countess I knew. She was Toscanini's favorite singer in Italy. This was the time of Mussolini. She did not leave Italy as many artists did. As a young woman, she was the richest young lady in Italy. Her mother was very society driven. She taught me how to cook a lot of Italian things! She loved to cook and they had a Cordon Bleu chef in their mansion and she would stick around the kitchen. It was the second or third year I was in Italy and I was doing films. One of her students, an Irishman, was studying voice with her. We were in a film together. In conversation, as we were waiting to go on, he recommended Countess Lisy as a voice teacher."

Lisy de Scalzi in her most famous role,
Cio Cio San in Madama Butterfly.

Wilkie gave me my career but she taught me where to put my voice. She called it la maschera—the mask. For opera projection, you had to have this very solid technique here in your voice, here in your head. Once it was in your maschera, you could shape it with whatever sound you wanted. We got to be personal friends. She was in her 80s at the time. We'd have her over to the house. Of course, that was very important to her because my husband was at the Embassy. She liked that. We were living in this villa. It didn't have tapestries from centuries ago but it was very nice. She had been reduced to living in a teeny tiny apartment. But she had some beautiful things. She showed me linens that were given to her from her mother which were given to her mother by the leader of Egypt for the opening of the Suez Canal. She was not personally there but her father and mother were. She had jewelry and all kinds of things that she was holding on to. She promised her students various things when she died. She didn't have children but she was married. She used to tell me the story that she personally went to Mussolini and begged for the life of her husband and Mussolini released her husband. She said, "I don't care what people say about Mussolini, he was always a very good friend of mine." Evidently, there was a social thing going on there, too. She was singing in Milano in contract with various companies. In your contract it specifies that you are allowed to sing so many days. It was five days. You had to give the voice a chance to rest. Her most famous role was Butterfly in Madame Butterfly. She's on stage virtually three hours and sings almost always, besides one or two interventions of the chorus. And so, she gets a note—"Mussolini politely asks for you to sing tonight in Butterfly". So she sends back a note, "Caro Duce, I've already sung my five shows and my one extra this week. I have to rest now". So she is in her apartment, at about 6 pm, and the performance let's say is around 9 pm, and two Carabinieri are at the door and they say, "Il Duce Aspetta and his car is outside". The car was sent to her to take her to the opera so she could perform that night. Screw your letter! She was about 4"11" and to be a Carabinieri you had to be 6'4'. It's a little scary. These two officers of the law, part of the army actually, take her down, put her in the car, and take her over to the theater. She was obliged to sing a performance personally for Mussolini. Her husband died and she remained a Countess. But sadly what happened was her brother came and took everything when she died. He knew that she had promised certain things to her students. He did give Dennis a few things. So Dennis called me and the other students and Dennis gave me a few silver objects from her. They are real Italian silver. One is a bread basket with a little cover. There are four or five pieces which he gave me. I treasure them. Oh there's a formaggiera, a cheese server. It's very old but beautiful."

"I did films. I did musicals. I did recordings. I wrote songs. I still get royalties all over the world from my songs which were in films. I had a big hit called Do it Do it Again with Raffaella Carra. You can see it on YouTube. Some

of the films are being shown in Brazil, or Panama and I still get paid for them even from films done in the 1970s. They have been very forceful in collecting the fees. For years and years, Russia would just take stuff. But the associations such as ASCAP in the US, the SIAE in Italy, etc. have an agreement with Russia now. The South American countries realize that they want to use some of our music and other countries want to use their music so they want their royalties, too. This agreement has happened within the last ten years. I'm always amazed about who's using my songs."

"Tony Cucchiara's agent got me a singing job in Dubai. (Richard was in Italy. Richard was working freelance writing little novels called Gialle. They are semi dirty novels but not pornographic or anything.) The restaurant owner, where I was singing, told me not to sit with anyone. Absolutely do not sit at the table of any of the patrons. They were always asking me to come to the table. Evidently, if I sat at the table a huge riot would ensue. So I understood. I didn't sit with anyone. The owner went away and said I've appointed the manager to take over for me for the week I'll be gone. Do what he says. So the first thing the manager does is tell me to sit at the table of one of the patrons. The next day a huge steam shovel appeared at the door of the restaurant and dug a huge hole so nobody could go into the restaurant. And it was a construction company who closed down the restaurant. When the owner came back he said to me, "Ann, what happened? Why did you sit with somebody?" I said, "The manager told me to." He said, "This is the worst thing that could have happened." The owner had to have the huge trench repaired. I left soon after. When I came back to Italy, Richard went to Saudi Arabia for one year and took Oliver with him and home schooled him. At that time, you could only work for the Embassy for five years. Suddenly, Richard was traveling to Africa, South Asia, and the Middle East, where he observed the 'beginning of the civil war in Lebanon, the start of the famine in sub-Saharan Africa, the last years of a brutal insurgency in Oman, and the events leading to the fall of the Shah and the capture of the American hostages in Iran.'"

Ann in Saudi Arabia.

"*I was recording with Giorgio Santini who had a recording studio in Rome. He knew the composer of the song Do It, Do It Again which Raffaella Carra sang. I was commissioned to write the lyrics in English. My words are not a translation. You can see it on YouTube in many languages and it was a hit in England (made popular by the Dr. Who series!). Giorgio and I tried to compose together but it was not successful. Giorgio started to show up at my house uninvited when Richard and I would have parties and he became a stalker. One of the things that got Richard so mad was Giorgio had an old Mercedes with a diesel engine and it made a loud putt putt sound. He would come over at night and drive around and around the house and that was really scary. I ignored his antics. I was invited to sing in Sardinia for the summer with a band. Giorgio wouldn't let me sing with a band so he had to make recordings so I could sing to the tracks. He convinced the producers that this was a good idea. Giorgio would just show up in Sardinia and the producer of one of the shows got so mad at Giorgio that he wouldn't pay me. He said that the people didn't like me singing to the playback. I was so angry. But on a funny note, every little town has their saint's day. This was the summer festival of this town. I had my playbacks, prerecorded music, and they had a raked stage in the piazza. There was a hale storm and the stage froze. I heard my music and I ran out on stage when suddenly my feet flew out from under me as I slipped onto my back with my legs straight up in the air. I start swooping down toward the audience! There was nothing to hang on to but I was able to stop just before the edge! I got up and the audience was roaring. They are applauding and laughing, "This is the best intro any performer has ever done!" I was so mortified! I did my number and they loved it. Afterward, there was a reception at the mayor's house. I didn't know if I should go or not. I thought they were going to arrest me! So I go to the mayor's house and they cheer, "You were wonderful! We loved it! What a great show!" I said, "That was a mistake, I slipped!" They said, "We thought that was part of the show!"*

"That summer of 1977, Richard left Italy and went to England to get his doctorate in political science at Oxford University's Oriel College. His focus was on contemporary European politics with a special focus on political violence. When Richard left I had a real fear of Giorgio. I got real anxiety. I tried to stay in my house but we had no money then and Richard couldn't send me any money to support the house and I really realized that I had to return to the US. What made it even more evident, Giorgio came to my house and knocked on the door one morning and when I opened the door he punched me in my face. I had been somewhere singing and I just got back. This is what cemented the fact that I should leave Rome. I gave our dog Woolfie to a friend and Oliver and I packed a bag. We got on a plane and went home to Buffalo. I left everything. Richard had the movers move everything to England. He had to wait till he had a house. He was just living in rooms till he could buy one. Richard was teaching political science for the University of Maryland."

"I enrolled Oliver in Frontier High School in Hamburg, NY. Jack Gallagher invited me to go to the St. Lawrence River where there was an oil spill and I wanted to see what that was all about and have that experience. I had known Jack since the Washington, D.C. days and I must have called him and told him I was home now. He has a big company that cleans up oil spills all over the world and he created the procedure to do so. Jack is a lawyer and an engineer so he created the patent for his invention. So I agreed to go and Oliver stayed in Buffalo at least a month with Mom and Dad. I learned how to clean after an oil spill. You virtually have to scrub every rock. You take the detergent and scrub every rock! And you have big trash bags to throw incidental rocks in. You have to clean the entire coast line. So Jack made me in charge of a group of women. They called me the mother mucker because mucking is what you do when you clean oil off the rocks. Well, the girls complained that I was like a prison matron. Eventually, we found out they didn't want to be in a girls group. The whole reason to be there was to meet guys! Not to seriously clean up the riverside! Although they did, they wanted to hang out with each other more than anything. So of course, I was very serious about cleaning the river. So, that didn't work at all! Jack took me off that job. I went out with another crew to clean the river. I was a good cleaner but I was not a good mother

*mucker! I was really struck by that. I thought I was doing such a good job!!
I personally liked the girls but I wasn't reading their intent. I helped clean
up the St. Lawrence Seaway!"*

"We moved to England then. Oliver and I joined Richard."

*Richard Collin, Ann Reid Collin, Oliver Collin, Penny Brown and her
friend Tony in front of Ann and Richard's home at Hugh Allen
Crescent in Oxford, England.*

*"Once I got settled in Oxford, England, I understood that Richard wanted
to become English or British and live in England full time. He did not*

want to return to the States. I realized there was no work that I could do there. At that time Actors Equity was fighting and not allowing any Brits to come to the US and Americans couldn't work. This was the late 70s. Since then they have come to an agreement. So I realized he was breaking off with me because he wanted to stay and I couldn't. When I left, we had an agreement that we were going to meet at his parents' house in Florida. But he never came. He sent Oliver. Oliver had a terrible time with his grandparents so I sent him a ticket to come to LA. Richard and I were childhood sweethearts and I always loved him. I always thought he was brilliant. We were divorced soon after I moved to Los Angeles. I need to rest again."

(Richard Collin has written academic articles on political violence and has conducted several interviews with actual terrorists. La Donna che Sparò a Mussolini [The Woman Who Shot Mussolini] was published in 1998 by Rusconi. Winter of Fire [a study of terrorism in Italy] was released by Dutton-Penguin in 1990. Imbroglio [a political novel] and Contessa [a story of love and politics in early twentieth-century Italy], were released in 1994 from St. Martin's Press. Richard's recent interest and writing involves the interconnection between languages and political conflict.)

In Los Angeles with Barry Jacobs, Mary, Pat Zaccarias,
Jack Repp (Ann's agent) Flash Reilly, Ann and Stephen Zaccarias.

Summertime at Beauty View Farm

Chee: June 2012

Ann was released from the rehab center in time for the big party planned at the farm over the 4th of July. During the summer of 2012 she was on maintenance dosages of chemo. I believe in all she got 3 rounds of chemo—the first was basically null and void because of the infection in her stomach. Summer of 2012 and early fall was when the serious talks of a Bone Marrow Transplant were discussed. Mary and I were tested but were not matches. Paul was not tested—too old! A couple donors were identified. Once it was concluded Ann was eligible for a BMT, donor found, tests done on Ann to make sure she could withstand the transplant, a date was set. Or was it?

Mary: It's the Fourth of July weekend! We decided to have a party and the whole family will meet at Beauty View Farm to support Ann, be with our mother and enjoy an old fashioned summer in Cattaraugus, NY in the Enchanted Mountains. My son, Rick, and his wife and son, Marla and Evan, join the fun from Valley Glen, CA. Ann's son, Oliver, and his wife, Rowena arrived from Van Nuys, CA. Chee and Mike with their children, Jim, Joe and Mikey drove in from Batavia, NY. My fiancé (now husband), Gino Gaudio, flew in from Burbank, CA. We enjoyed the Buffalo Philharmonic at the base of the ski hill in Ellicottville, NY. The music was so patriotic and uplifting. There were red, white and blue flags everywhere—on mailboxes, lamp posts and gazebos. Local musicians set the mood throughout the village. On top of Snyder Hill where Beauty View Farm is located, there was swimming in the acre pond, pizza in the pizza oven and hiking all over our 425 acre family farm. It's been in the family for over 160 years so there's lots of history in this part of the country. It was Gino's first time at the farm. It was just a year ago I was at the farm without Gino. While talking on our cell phones, I was walking along the road listening to the frogs in the pond croaking away and I teasingly asked him if this city boy was afraid of frogs. You know, the sounds of the country can keep people awake and terrify them. He responded, "No, just bears." I laughed so hard!

He's fitting right in and enjoying making his famous pizza in the pizza oven. Everyone crowded around to see the master at work. The best thing to do is to find all the organic, fresh ingredients you can find. It's so delicious! It's so good I think I have to share the recipe with you:

Pizza Recipe

5 cups flour
2 cups water
1 packet of yeast
1 teaspoon sugar
Mozzarella
1 pound of organic heirloom tomatoes
2 cans of plum tomatoes
2 cans of tomato sauce
2 cans of tomato paste
2 cans of water
Garlic
Green onions
Excellent Italian olive oil only
Sea salt
Black pepper

Basil leaves for the topping
Corn meal

First you take a cup of warm water and combine the yeast and ½ teaspoon of sugar until it foams. Mix flour and yeast water with a teaspoon of olive oil and salt. Knead till dough is smooth and pliable to the touch. If you press into the dough and make a dimple, the dimple will rise. Let the dough sit and rise in a warm place for a couple of hours. For the sauce you put some olive oil in the bottom of your kettle. Add 2 chopped green onions and a clove of chopped garlic and sauté in the bottom of the pan until translucent. Take the plum tomatoes and hand crush them. Add to the kettle with the tomato sauce and paste. Now add the water. Heat the sauce and add salt and pepper to taste. Let it simmer for a couple hours. Now to make the pizza pies, roll the dough with a rolling pin to create a very thin pie. Pinch the edges around the circumference of the pie to form a crust. Rub olive oil over the top. Add a layer of tomato sauce, thin slices of mozzarella and slices of heirloom tomatoes. Use corn meal to slide the pizza into the oven with a pizza paddle. The oven should be 800 degrees. Cook for 3 minutes or till golden brown. Top with fresh basil leaves. Devour quickly before a creature steals it from you.

Gino was having a great time throwing the pizza in the air and our 94 year old mother was clapping her hands and calling out "Speech, speech!" Of course, he obliged and shared a lovely speech. She was like a child enjoying all the festivities around her even if she didn't know any of us. She did recognize that Gino was very handsome.

We're making Gino's famous pizza.

As I stated earlier, Gino's known my family for twenty-five years. When Ann toured with Pirates of Penzance, Ann would watch Gino's daughter, Gratci, when his wife was on stage. When the tour was done and they returned to Los Angeles Ann continued composing music and she would recruit us to sing in her productions. This was when she started her work on "AElinor of Acquitaine". Ann has been working on AElinor for many years, trying to get it to a level where she's comfortable to submit it to production companies. She traveled through Europe and visited sites where AElinor lived and did extensive research on the characters. She's expanded her music writing horizons and composed music for my quartet called Spring LA, a piano piece celebrating our ancestors, and a musical to help save the blue birds in New York State.

Beauty View Farm bought tickets for the Ellicottville Chamber of Commerce Fourth of July Events and we all went to the base of Holiday Valley Ski Area to hear the Buffalo Philharmonic play patriotic music and watch fireworks. A delicious dinner was served, too. It was a warm, balmy summer night and everyone was so happy lying on the grass, looking up at the stars which were so close you could almost touch them. The stars are always brilliant in the country. There's no extra light to defuse the starlight. Ann was very happy to be out in the world with us and not cooped up in the rehab home. We were so happy she lived through the first part of her strenuous ordeal.

On our way home, Gino wanted to drive and Paul and I were telling him to watch out for the deer. They like to leap out of the woods right in front of your car. These deer have a knack for that, they're trained stealth deer. Gino was driving very earnestly and intensely. In the mean time, a car in front of us was swerving quite a bit. Finally, the car made a left turn and got out of our way. The next thing we know, flashing lights are pulling up quickly behind us. Gino pulled over immediately. "Where you from?" asked the NY State Trooper as he sauntered up to the car. Gino and I said, "Los Angeles, CA." Paul said, "I live in Cattaraugus on Snyder Hill Road." The officer asked each of us for our licenses. Then he told Gino to get out of the car. "Can I ask why?" Gino inquired. "You were swerving back there. Have you been drinking?" inquired the officer. "I had a glass of wine with dinner around 5:00 PM. Nothing since then" said Gino. It was around 11:00 PM and the officer made Gino blow in the breathalyzer and do the walk but there was no need. The officer let us go but we could tell he was very disappointed that he wasn't able to make an arrest. It would have been big money! Now our plan is to buy a place in town so we don't have to drive all the way back to the farm after an Ellicottville event. (It is only twenty minutes away.) Or at least rent a place when we're there in the summer or winter so all our kids can enjoy both the farm and Ellicottville. Maybe stay in town and swim in the pool and play golf in the summer and of course ski in the winter. Then head to the farm and make pizza in the pizza oven, paddle boat, hike and just lounge. What a life!

New York City Professional Dancers

Ann's back in the hospital again—more chemo to prepare her for the Bone Marrow Transplant (BMT). It's hair loss time. She cut it off because she was losing so much very quickly. At this point, Ann was interested in wearing scarves. Roswell people helped her find some beautiful, colorful scarves that helped her feel cute and sexy. A group of professional dancers from NYC visited patients in the hospital and they were introduced to Ann. She was very excited and encouraged by their work. She had her computer with her and played the ballet that she composed for AElinor and told the dancers her story. AElinor was married to King Louis of France and they went on a crusade to the Holy Land. They took separate boats and ended up losing each other. King Louis was shipwrecked and Queen AElinor's ship was taken over by Nur-al-Din, the Arab king. There was a flirtation and the dance between the two leaders ensued. The dance troupe decided to create a dance specifically for Ann and they performed it in her room. Ann was in the news and had an article written about her. The dance troupe paid for the arts in the hospital and Ann was a participant. She also learned how to play a ukulele!

This is one of Ann's Art Therapy lessons when she was at Roswell Park Cancer Institute.

Ann closed her eyes, with visions of Broadway swirling in her head. She told me, "I would love to be on Broadway still! Oh what a beautiful dream this is. It's amazing seeing my ballet being performed by a professional dance troupe. It was wonderful meeting the marvelous dancers and being inspired by them. They came to my room and choreographed their ballet to my music. I believe it really helped me heal because I was in such a positive, euphoric state of mind! I see myself sitting in the front row just happy as a lark watching the dancers tell my story, or rather the story of Queen AElinor of Aquitane and Henry Plantagenet of England. Who would I like to play Henry? How about Hugh Jackman? He was wonderful in Les Miserables! And Ann Hathaway could play AElinor although AElinor is ten to fifteen years older than Henry. Who's a British or Australian female singer who could keep up with Hugh Jackman? What about Lea Michele from Glee as AElinor and a twenty year old young pop star to play Henry? Justin Bieber? Ha Ha! Lea Michele would whip him into shape. I'd really like Mariette Hartley to play the narrator who is AElinor in her 80s. Or, oh, oh Vanessa Redgrave!!!!"

Mary: How many times has she been admitted to the hospital now? I'm losing track. We're back in for another round of chemo. They have to make sure all the leukemia is out of her before the bone marrow transplant. And they found someone! Another young man, he's 25 years old. Maybe he'll give Ann a shot of youth to help her overcome everything she's going through!

In October 2012 we found out that the bone marrow transplant would take place but Ann had to have all of her caregivers committed to a specific schedule. Her friend, Jack, was going to be the first one to stay with her at Hope Lodge. Hope Lodge is a non-profit organization that helps people recover from cancer and it's close to the hospital in case there's a relapse. We all started making plans on who could be there for her and when. We worked it out so that Ann's daughter-in-law, Rowena, would be the second caregiver, Oliver would be the third one, I would be the fourth one and Chee would be last. Each of us would be with her for two weeks and we would all have to learn how to do all kinds of nurse things. It was very scary for those of us who never have done anything like this! Ann, Paul, Chee and I talked about not knowing anything about caring for other people when we started being caregivers for our mom. First of all, it's our mother and she didn't want her children to see her weaknesses. Then she would say, "This is what old looks like." As her dementia kicked in, we noticed she had different things that she would do to make each one of us crazy. Ann's irritant was when mom would pick at her skin and dig holes in her arms and make them bleed. Paul couldn't stand it when mom would scrape the table with her nails. She would look at me and say, "You're starting to get some wrinkles." I said to her, "Yes I know and you have lots." Chee didn't have anything that bugged her. She told mom to dig and scrape away. Anyway, we all started making travel arrangements and tried to work it into our vacation days.

The Phone Rang Again, Now What...

Chee's version, October 2012

Ann needed round-the-clock caregivers for days 30-100 after the transplant. (The first 30 days she would be at Roswell.) Also, a facility had to be found for her to stay at since both Batavia and Cattaraugus were too far away. Her caseworker was working on a facility and it turned out to be Hope Lodge; Ann was working on getting her caregivers lined up. Ann's friend Jack was going to be her primary caregiver. He flew to Buffalo in early October to attend the caregiver training. Me, our friend Liz and my son Joe could fill in. Mary, son Oliver and daughter-in-law Rowena, all in California, could be called in if necessary. Then the proverbial shit hit the fan! Jack's daughter-in-law called Roswell and said he was too old and feeble to act as Ann's caregiver. Roswell cancelled the BMT until these issues could be resolved.

Mary:

Wait . . . . This news was very alarming and frustrating. Jack's daughter-in-law didn't want Jack to be involved so she called Roswell Institute and told them that Jack was incompetent. She's a nurse so she carries some pull in the medical field and they believed her. The transplant was off.

Boy was I pissed! I was so angry but Ann didn't want me to call the bitch. She basically just killed my sister. I thought about it and realized Ann didn't say I couldn't talk to Jack. He had a right to know what his daughter-in-law just did. So I emailed him and he called me immediately. He was livid! He wanted her out of his life. The only person who could say he was incompetent was his primary doctor. His whole life could have changed if Jack would have let her get away with this. He wouldn't be able to travel, lecture, or continue his work. Jack was finally able to turn this around by having his doctor call Roswell but the bone marrow transplant was still cancelled. Roswell also decided to put an age limit on caregivers.

We got on the phone and everyone was able to re-arrange their schedules and suddenly the transplant was on again and it was scheduled a week later! We were so fortunate that the donor didn't change his mind. Our friend Liz Kraengel, who's also our lawyer for the farm, stepped up along with Chee's son Joe (studying to be a veterinarian at the time) and they stayed with Ann the first few days when Chee couldn't be there. Jack was able to help at the end when Ann was on the mend. He became the last caregiver and they were able to enjoy time together without worrying about doing something horribly wrong nurse-wise like giving the wrong meds or changing tubing wrong for intravenous meds! Oliver, Rowena and I were able to be there throughout December and part of January. What a relief! What an ordeal!

Chee's thoughts, October 2012

Donor number 2 was lined up. Ann scrambled to get her caregivers scheduled, and her caseworker was able to secure Hope Lodge for her post BMT days. The BMT was scheduled for the end of October. Rowena would come right after Thanksgiving, about Day 30; Oliver would come next; Mary after Oliver; and Jack (situation resolved) would come for the final stay. Once again, Liz, Joe and I

would be backup. The three of us attended a care giver seminar on November 12. They promised pizza but it was all gone by the time we got there. We each did get a can of pop, though.

October 18, 2012

I drove Ann to Roswell Park so they could begin the pre-BMT procedures. We arrived about 7:00 AM. For the next 5 days Ann would receive massive amounts of chemo to kill as much of her bone marrow as possible (they can't kill it all). Day 6 would be a day of rest (ha, ha, no chemo but more tests) and Day 7 would be BMT Day, or back to Day Zero! After I got Ann all settled in, I left Roswell about 10:00 AM. I drove back to Batavia, picked up my mother-in-law to drive back to Buffalo for a follow-up appointment for her recent glaucoma surgery. When I got back to my office at 3:30 PM my husband asked "Is the medical transport service done for the day?"

October 25, 2012 — BMT Day!

Mary:

We're all a little, no, a lot nervous about the actual transplant. How will Ann's body absorb this foreign DNA? Will she reject it? Will her body be strong enough to survive? She's had so much chemo it's hard to imagine what more her body can take. Ann was resting up for her new DNA that will be injected into her body. Now she will consist of two different DNA! The field of science is amazing! The only thing Ann can do is reminisce about her life.

She day dreams, telling me more, "I moved to Los Angeles and got a job with the show "Pirates of Penzance" with Pam Dauber and Jim Belushi. They were the stars in this production. I got the job in "Pirates of Penzance" actually due to the influence of the musical director in Hair, Bill Elliot. He really wanted me in the show for my voice so I became a Booth Baby. I was never supposed to go on stage. Others are trained to go on stage. They paid us full pay so they could keep the integrity of the part. I thought this was outstanding. That was Joe Papp's idea and he was the producer, first class. He produced the New York Shakespeare Festival and "A Chorus Line" which started out in a church and then it moved to Broadway. Then he produced "Pirates of Penzance" which ran on Broadway with Linda Ronstadt and Kevin Klein. I was in the first National Tour. Bill Elliot did the brilliant orchestrations where he substituted the strings for the xylophone. All of the tempos were much faster and it was a very happy sound. They also pushed the funny factor. Everyone loved it and would stand in line to see the show several times! So Bill Elliot was responsible for helping me get Pirates. I was hired to go on when Diane Benedict delivered her baby, Gratci, and they kept me on afterward. I used to carry Gratci around a lot when Diane was doing something else. Jim Belushi came by and said you have the most beautiful breasts. At the time it made me so mad! My one encounter with the guy and he said this! And I liked Belushi in the part! I liked him, he was like the street gang character while others had been the gentleman. You know, very British, very gentleman like pirate king. Jim was your Brooklyn street pirate king. But he was just as effective, with his singing and his schtick. I thought he was very good. He and Pam were excellent together. Her singing was amazing with her pop quality and the high notes. Pam was very formal and very nice. She invited us all to a Christmas dinner at a restaurant. During the time I was in the show, one of the Gibb brothers, Andy, played the boy lead. He was in love with Victoria Principal. She left him and he committed suicide. We weren't told the story of what happened but that was the first traumatic event that occurred during the show. I have to say about that production—every night I listened to the singing and it was gorgeous. I never got tired of the show. There were grandmas, teenagers . . . everybody loved the show. Many people came back three to four times. It was so much fun to be so appreciated. We were on tour when John Belushi died. It was terrible. Jim had to leave the show and go to Chicago. The mother was stricken and Jim had to go to be with her. The administration was very understanding. I think a Cassidy brother took over when Jim was gone. When the show closed, everyone auditioned to go to NY and I didn't because I wanted to stay in Los Angeles. I did go to see the show in NY and one of my friends said, "Oh Ann, it's so natural to see you back here." For a moment I felt like I should have auditioned and gone to NY. That's one thing I haven't done. A show on Broadway! Now I say I'm going to make it big on Broadway when I'm 80. Some big show will come up and I'll be in it! Actually, Pippen involves the grandmother and she has a big song. I'm keeping that in mind. Maybe I'll write the show that goes to Broadway."

Le Parnasse

Ann and Mary Reid
Composers Connection
(213) 436-9092

*Ann played keyboards and I played flute in restaurants in
Los Angeles at this time in our lives.*

"I conducted Pirates in a dinner theater in Orange County and Alex Daniels played the pirate king. He was a wonderful pirate king but he kept getting hurt all the time. He would thoroughly immerse himself into the character! He was extremely effective as a pirate king. Alex would throw himself off the stage and he'd bounce back up off the trampoline. He was hilarious! He did such a good job in the show! He was also a very talented musician. He sang so well and played the trombone! Remember at our Christmas party? Now he's a famous stunt coordinator. He choreographed the howling funny wrestling scene in Borat and the girl twerking prank on the Jimmy Kimmel show. That's Dafney, Brian Thomas' daughter who is becoming a star stunt woman. Remember Brian and Alex both worked with you in the Conan the Barbarian Show at Universal Studio? Brian was also in Cobra and Jason and the Argonauts."

"When I was in Italy, we would be invited to people's homes after the show and they were the aristocracy but they were so unhappy. It was a lesson to me. What is happiness? It's not an ancient villa 400 years old. It's not all the money you have—the nouveau riche. I look at my life: my little house in Van Nuys; my farm; my teaching experience in Batavia, NY and I'm just happy. I moved to Batavia because I had to have a total hysterectomy and I was really worried about health care. It got all infected. Hey that's the first time my abdomen got infected. It cost over $50,000.00 and the month before I had purchased insurance through my union and they paid everything. I had the weirdest gut instinct that I better get insurance, I better get insurance. It cost me $500.00 per month and I was virtually unemployed. I was working for a lawyer part-time. Then Chee called me and said there's a job in music in Batavia. You should apply for it.

Me, Ann and Chee when Ann was thinking of moving to Batavia, NY.

I did and I was one of the people invited for interviews and they looked at my resume and said, "You'll never stay here." I said, "OK, I'll give you five years." Of course, I was there 17 years. I really loved it! I thought I'd have all the time in the world. I'd write all my shows and audition for shows in Buffalo and NYC. The work was just so much—I had 5 classes a semester plus the musical which I had to conduct and arrange because we could never afford the 22 orchestra members it was written for. And I had to change keys and play the synthesizer half the time. I had to mouth the words because the students would always get screwed up! Many of them had never been in shows in high school or anything. You have to have that attitude. You have to say "let's do it" because you're training these people to go on to college. We had some success stories with students working on cruise ships, trying out for Broadway shows, stuff like that."

"When I started teaching I thought that I would lecture and everybody would listen with their mouths open because it was so interesting. It took me awhile to realize that their eyes were just glazed over! I didn't know

what to do! So I decided that they would teach the course. Not me. I assigned people projects. Or they chose themselves. The whole idea was that they had to have a project with music and video plus they had to talk about their subject which included the composer of the period and their music, of course. It was a big thing and it would take the whole period. Oh boy did they moan and groan about that. But it was really good for them and I was speaking to one of my students one day and I said, "Ok, what did you learn in this course?" And she said, "I only learned what my subject was." And I laughed, hallelujah! She learned something! She mastered it, too. She had to stand up in front of the class, have her videos ready, talk about the music and play it. You have to prepare and if you don't show up the day of the presentation you get an F. Practically everyone showed up! Sometimes they'd ask me if they could make it up, or present on another day, and I said well you start with a B not an A. I used all of the modalities in my teaching, too. One of my students couldn't sit still and had to walk around the classroom. We talked about the personal style of learning. Some people can read it in books. I can't do that. I have to have a teacher or someone play it for me or I have to see it. There are learners who have to go off by themselves or there are those that have to be in a group. Then there was the kinesthetic learner who has to move all the time. Well, in one of my classes, I had this big, attractive African American young man from NYC. He would walk up and down and shout things pertaining to the class I was teaching from the back of the room and walk around between the other students. I took away the whole thing of sitting in rows and I had tables like a seminar. The students were so pissed off with this guy. He was talking all the time but I recognized that he was always contributing to what we were learning. He had obviously read the material while the other students hadn't. So he was doing really well and had good grades. He had trouble doing his presentation. He came to me and didn't know what to do. During our talk he revealed to me that he had been in prison and as a youth done all the bad stuff that he could think of. The only thing that saved him was that somebody in prison recognized how intelligent he was and how interested he was in stuff that he didn't know about. This guy introduced him to books, art and this guy convinced him that he could go to college. This man supervised him in taking the GED and my student ended up in Batavia surrounded by pastures and cows with certain smells wafting in the breezes. He told me that he was getting good grades in everything he was taking except math. So they got him a math tutor and he got through it. So a few years later he shows up dressed to the nines in an officer's uniform of the US army. He was now a dentist! The army had made him a dentist!! Which was perfect for him, he could walk around and wasn't forced to sit still. They saw his potential! He was so proud. He was an officer, probably a Lieutenant and a doctor of dentistry. Oh, what an accomplishment! I saw his intelligence and the fact that he had to move all the time didn't bother me because we talked about this in professional development. Wow, am I ever feeling better! Hi Chee!" Chee walked in her room with the next bit of news.

The Phone Rang, Come on now, Really!

Chee's thoughts: Things go well. In fact, things go so well for Ann that they want to release her from Roswell about Day 21, versus 30. NOOOO!!! But her caregivers are lined up for Day 30!!!! That's nine days with no one lined up!

November 13

Ann was released from Roswell. I was able to juggle work and family schedule to cover until Rowena arrived in town, about November 26. I was with Ann from November 13-November 16. Then friend Liz and my son Joe stepped in to help out the weekend of November 16-19.

Monday, November 19

A group from GM (General Motors) brought a Thanksgiving Dinner for residents and caregivers. My son Jim from Las Vegas was in Buffalo so he joined us for dinner with Ann, Joe, and me. Jim stayed with Joe in Buffalo. Joe gave Jim a few bucks to go to the DMV, get his motorcycle permit, and he gave it to Joe for fake id. Nice to see the brothers working together on something!

Thursday, November 22

We spent Thanksgiving at Hope Lodge. In the morning Ann and I walked to the corner of Summer Street and Delaware Avenue to watch the Turkey Trot (oldest continually run footrace in North America—5 months older than the Boston Marathon!). A resident's wife cooked up a Thanksgiving feast! Joining Ann and me for Thanksgiving dinner were Joe, my husband Mike and daughter Mikey Kate (she'll be staying through the weekend), our brother Paul and Mom from Cattaraugus. Paul dropped Mom off at Hope Lodge before dinner and headed to Lockport—to pick up his friend Mike (who's going back to Cattaraugus with them.) But here comes another problem!

Paul's car broke down in Lockport-engine seized up! My husband Mike left Hope Lodge and picked up Paul and Mike in Lockport. (Paul left his car in Lockport to be fixed by a friend.) After dinner, Paul drove friend Mike and Mom back to Cattaraugus in Ann's car. Paul needed to have the car back by Monday, November 26 so I can pick Rowena up from the airport. All is understood.

During my stay at Hope Lodge my friend Sue Penepent visited Ann at Hope Lodge from the North Country (she's in town for relatives in Buffalo.) She's a visiting nurse and remembers doing some training at Hope Lodge (training rooms are in the basement for the American Cancer Society.) Also, our cousin Ron from Churchville visited for a couple hours. He was a little perplexed about me having to stay with Ann around the clock. "Don't you have a job?" "Don't you have a family?" Yes, but you do what you need to do!

Monday, November 26

Another organization brought dinner for the residents and caregivers at Hope Lodge. AND Paul has to get Ann's car back to Buffalo! Joe joined in the dinner and Paul arrived about 7 PM. I drove Paul back to Cattaraugus (one hour), then back to Hope

Lodge (another hour back.) Joe stayed with Ann while I was gone. That night, there was some tree trimming and games played at Hope Lodge. I asked how that went but Joe and Ann did not participate. Apparently, the magnesium infusion machine was acting up, kept buzzing that there was a problem so they went up to Ann's room to see if they could figure it out. I left about 11:30 PM to pick Rowena up from the airport. I arrived back at Hope Lodge about 12:45 PM. What a night!

Tuesday, November 27

I'm relieved of my caregiving duties! Rowena takes over.

I believe Joe drove Rowena to the airport and picked up Oliver. Christmas was spent at Beauty View Farm. When my family arrived at the farm for Christmas, I commented on how nice the great room looked—furniture moved around, most of the clutter out of the way. I didn't know that Ann tripped over something and there was a big blow-up between Oliver and Paul! The blow-up was over each one taking care of their mothers—Paul with our mom and Oliver with our sister. It's best not to know all the details sometimes.

Mary: Now it's my turn to take over the caregiver duties. I'm due to arrive the night after Christmas. I wanted to spend Christmas with my son's family, Rick, Marla, Evan and Juliet—Gino and his family—Gratci, Bobby and the boys, Ryan and Evan plus Gemma, Eric and Gino's sister Nina. When you travel to the east coast in the winter, you always have to stay relaxed and fluid. This happened to be a rather snowy winter so when I arrived in Chicago (Grrrr I always get stuck there) all the flights were cancelled into Buffalo. Naturally, it had to be expected. It was late, probably midnight, and I convinced the airline people that I had to get to Hope Lodge to take care of my sister who just had a Bone Marrow Transfer. They were very kind and got me on an early flight out to Rochester, NY. ☺ So I slept in the airport ☹ Poor Chee had to drive all the way to Rochester to pick me up and then drive me to Hope Lodge in Buffalo. Oliver completed his time with his mother so he jumped in the car and Chee took him to the airport. Chee finally got to go home and rest. In the meantime, I'm learning about all these nurse things I need to do and I'm terrified. I'm not a nurse! I don't like this stuff! Every medication has to be taken in a specific way so you really had to be on a schedule and know what time it was and what day it was. No goofing off! Breakfast, lunch and dinner had to be extremely regimented. I ventured out into the snow drifts and banks and bought food at the local store around the corner. The kitchen had lots of counter space. Exciting! Great for cooking! It also had two dish washers, two refrigerators and lots of cupboard space. You had to put your name on all your food or someone would eat it. But that's how it is with communal living. People liked to tell their stories while you were preparing a meal so it was very therapeutic and helpful to learn about all the processes that the patients went through to get to this survival state. Ann and I cooked together, watched TV and read books. We had talked about selling some of the hardwood trees at the farm and redoing the kitchen since our family was expanding with new grandchildren and partners. I found an architect while searching the internet in Los Angeles and made an appointment to meet him in Buffalo. It turned out that he had a cabin near our farm so we decided to meet him at the farm instead and he could see if this project would be interesting to him. It was very cold and there was quite a bit of snow all around so Chee picked us up at Hope Lodge. Mikey decided to grace us with her presence. We love hanging out with Mikey. At thirteen years old, she has great taste in music and clothing. Plus she's smart, funny and interesting. Cattaraugus and Ellicottville were beautiful, all snowy and pretty like villages under a Christmas tree.

Chee, Mikey and me are in cold and snowy Ellicottville.
We love to shop here after the farm.

We turned right after the sucker stick factory onto Waite Hollow Road.
Chee was on the phone with Paul to see if the architect arrived yet
and I was on the phone with the architect to see if he was lost yet! Just
after the railroad tracks (where Aunt Victoria's model T was hit by a
train and she became an invalid so Mr. Rich divorced her) Chee's car
started slipping and sliding all over. We couldn't make it up the hill! At
that moment Ann announced she desperately had to pee. She got out
of the car as Chee and I are trying to see if someone can come get us.
Mikey was the only one who saw Ann fall and she yelled, "Aunt Annie
fell in the snow bank!" We see her sliding down the hill on the ice!
Chee and I ran over to help her up and pull her back together. Never
a dull moment! John Lydon, the architect, was kind enough to come
down the hill and rescue us. Theresa, mom's caregiver, was also at the
house and she helped figure out the situation. We left Chee's car at the
sucker stick factory and Theresa brought us back. What an ordeal! The

meeting with John Lydon was very successful and exciting though. We got some great ideas for the remodel and he seemed to understand the look we want. We all decided to hire him to do the drawings. The next step is to harvest the trees and see how much money we can make from the sale. These are good projects to keep Ann occupied and instill in her the will to live.

We really couldn't do too much. Not even walk around the neighborhood in Buffalo. There was lots of snow on the sidewalk and it was too difficult to maneuver. In spite of it all, Ann was progressing nicely. She was in good spirits. I would go to Roswell with Ann for her doctor appointments and during one of our excursions we found out that the American Cancer Society gave patients free wigs! So a very nice woman helped Ann try on wigs and we found one that fit her perfectly. She looked so cute and happy.

Ann's new look!

We took a ride to Batavia and checked in on her house, saw Chee and had lunch at a charming café. Things were moving forward. She was also very happy about her relationship with her daughter-in-law, Rowena. Rowena took such good care of Ann. Ann said that this was Rowena's calling.

My time with Ann was up. Jack was on his way to Buffalo and Hope Lodge via Washington, DC. Ann and I picked him up at the airport and all was well. They've known each other 40 years. Now they planned on going over old times and spending valuable time together. Ann was released from Hope Lodge and Jack took her to Batavia to move back into her home. She needed to spend time organizing her things because all of her belongings from her work office were brought to her home. Stacks of books and boxes were strewn all over her living room and bedrooms. It was so overwhelming! We were also closing out our mom's house and selling it. We were in the process of sorting through all of our mom's cherished items. It was heartbreaking because our dad built the house where we grew up for our mom. All of our childhood memories were made there. All we can do is hope the new owner will take care of the house the way our dad did. To us it had magical healing powers. Whenever we were exhausted or beat up by the world, we could go home and recover, regroup and relax. I would take Rick home to Buffalo at least twice a year and we'd make pumpkins for Halloween, my mom's famous kuchen for Christmas and every summer we'd go to the Erie County Fair, one of the largest in the country. There was no more going home now. This part of our lives would now be over. No parents to take care of us when we were down and out. Now everything had to go to the farm. We can only afford to keep one property and the farm has been in the family for over 150 years so we have to put our time and attention into keeping it for our children and grandchildren. It's so difficult making decisions about stuff. Do we keep it? Toss it? Love it? Is it valuable? Is it sentimental? Ann has to go through her own things, as well, and make these tough decisions.

The Phone Rang…oh no, Mom or Ann

Chee: February 13, 2013

Mom had a "heart episode" and was transported to Lakeshore Hospital in Irving. Doctors said, "There doesn't seem to be anything wrong, her heart is just "old"." Ann and I discussed and decided to proceed with her getting a pacemaker. Surgery took place on her 96th birthday, February 16. Ann visited Mom in the hospital a few times. She was released a couple days after the surgery.

The Phone Rang, Meow Meow!

Friday, March 1, 2013

Chee's version:

Ann has been back in Batavia for a few weeks. Things seem to be going smoothly, or about as smoothly as can be expected. She had an appointment at Roswell on Tuesday, February 26 and everything was all in check. The weather was cold and dreary all week. I spoke to Ann every day and she was saying she was cold. I said everyone is cold. It's that wet, dreary cold that seems to penetrate your soul! I told her to make sure her thermostat was turned up—now was not the time to be frugal. I did not physically see Ann, just spoke with her every day. Antonio, a Burke Parkway friend of Ann's, called Mike at our office about 4:15 PM. He said he was concerned about Ann, she wasn't making any sense and he just got off the phone with her. All she kept saying was "I'm cold". Mike asked me if I should go check on her. I begrudgingly said I would, but I had talked to her this morning. I went to Ann's house, rang the doorbell and pounded on the door. No answer. I called Ann—she answered. I told Ann to come down and let me in. Ann hung up. I pounded on the door some more, called Ann and she hung up again. I called Mike to put him on notice that he may have to come and help me (I did not want to have to break the glass to get in, but would if it's the last resort.) I called

Ann again and told Ann to stay on the line and come down and let me in. Ann finally did. Ann's bedroom was in disarray. Pills were all over the floor. Ann was disoriented. I called Roswell-they instructed me to take Ann to UMMC Hospital (in Batavia, one block from Ann's house). I did and I brought with me all the instructions about being a BMT, special precautions to take, etc. Ann was extremely disoriented, she didn't remember anything. I did the best I could to reconstruct a time frame. After tests and communication with Roswell they decided to transport her. EMT's arrived about 11:30 PM, prepared her for transport and she headed off to Roswell. Selfish me! After months of running around for Ann and Mom and keeping my schedule open for last minute problems, Mike and I were going to go out to dinner with friends this Friday night. So much for those plans!

March 2, 2013

Mike and I participated in the Old First Ward Shamrock run. The starting line was about three-quarters of a mile from Roswell Park. Our activities were: first, we drove to Buffalo's west side and took a photo of Antonio's property on Rhode Island Street for insurance purposes; stopped into Roswell to see Ann about 9:30 AM—no prognosis yet from the doctors—too early in the morning—she was still incoherent, and meowing! The nurses, doctors, and staff don't know what to think of that! Mike and I ran (in my case briskly walked) the 8K course; had a quick beer; stopped back at Roswell to check on Ann (still no diagnosis yet but they are running all kinds of tests); picked Joe up at his place in Buffalo; had some wings at the Anchor Bar (Joe got a drink at the bar. Joe got to use the fake ID Jim got him in November. What a nice brother); dropped Joe off; then back to Batavia.

Conclusion: Ann had a very severe urinary tract infection—it was septic—it was affecting her brain. This affects people's brains. Now the doctors brought in special infectious disease doctors to figure out what antibiotic to use. The one they agreed upon costs about $6,000 per round!

March 12, 2013

Ann was released from Roswell. I picked her up and the plan was to go back to the farm right away. Paul has been on vacation for the last week so Mom's caregivers have been staying overnight to watch Mom (24 hour coverage). Ann and I were going to relieve them. Roswell wanted Ann back at 6:00 AM the next morning for tests. I was quite peeved—if I had known I would have recommended Ann stay at Hope Lodge, then go the next morning for tests, etc. then up to the Farm. We went to the farm and left at 5:00 AM the next morning for Roswell. I got peeved again and had to leave the examination room when the nurse asked if there was anyone who could organize Ann's pills for her! If she was incompetent to manage her pills at this point why was she released! The appointment was over so Ann and I headed back to the farm and I returned to Batavia. Exhausted!

During the course of the next month Ann noticed Mom was not recovering from her heart episode. I had been going to the farm on weekends and noticed Mom's deteriorating condition as well. She seemed to have lost the will to carry on. We made her as comfortable as possible. Ann was in contact with Hills Funeral Home to discuss costs and procedures so we are prepared.

April 8, 2013

I took out Mom's stock folder. I thought that some, or all, of the stock may have to be sold to cover increased costs in caregiving—more hours and more expertise needed. Also, we may need to get a medical bed, medical chair, etc. to make things easier for mom and her caregivers. Lastly, we may need to pay people to watch Mom while we're all out in LA for Mary's wedding. As an alternative she could go to a hospice or similar place while we're gone. Value of the stock is about $24,000. I will talk to everyone later in the week about selling some of the stock.

April 10, 2013

At about 4:15 PM, Ann called me and said, "I think that's it for Mom." I said "I know, Mom's lost her will, she slumps in her chair." Ann said, "No Chee, I think that's it for Mom." Mom had died. Ann called Hills Funeral Home. I left Batavia and headed to Cattaraugus. I passed Mom's hearse on the corner of Markham Road and Route 353. Time 6:45 PM.

The Phone Rang, R.I.P Maribell

Mary: This is the worst phone call. The one you dread. I thought she would make it to our wedding but Ann and Chee were warning me that she was deteriorating quickly but no matter how old they are, you still think you have more time. Even if she didn't always know who I was, she had those moments of remembering and she would say so in such a unique, funny way. You just had to laugh. Our cute, sweet mom was gone.

Rick and Grandma Maribell the night before his wedding. She was 94.

Chee's thoughts: Ann and I started working on arranging a memorial service for Mom, coordinating time with LA folk. Everything has seemed to calm down, everyone is moving forward. BUT THEN:

The Phone Rang!

April 19, 2013

It's about 4:15 PM, I was wandering around Bed, Bath, and Beyond scouting out bargains and I got a call from Ann. But wait, it wasn't Ann, it was a Marshal from the Cattaraugus Indian Reservation letting me know Ann was in a car accident and was being transported via ambulance to Lakeshore Hospital in Irving. I spoke to Ann briefly and said I'd see if Paul or Theresa (one of Mom's caregivers) could go there (I'm a 2 hour drive away.) I called Paul and lo and behold, Theresa was at the farm. Theresa drove to the hospital in Irving to be with Ann. After numerous x-rays, CT scans, and MRIs it was concluded nothing was broken, she was just banged up a lot. Ann was released and Theresa drove her back to Cattaraugus. The car was totaled.

April 20, 2013

Lois the visiting nurse was at the Farm. Ann was in great pain so it was decided she was to go to Springville Hospital for additional tests. The ambulance was called and Ann was transported. Conclusion, nothing was broken, just banged up a lot.

Ann continued her recovery. Urinary tract infection seems to be under control. Time can only heal her from the car accident. It was

decided that Ann should go to LA over winter and be with her son and daughter-in-law. It was not in her best interest to live alone for the time being.

Ann and I worked on the logistics for Mom's Memorial Mass the upcoming summer. Also, we needed to get the apartment ready for guests via the Amish Trail, Craigslist, Airbnb, etc. Theresa, Paul, and Ann worked on this. Our first guests arrived on Memorial Day Weekend! This was working out well and it gave Ann something to do rather than focus on her illnesses. She had to make sure the beds were made, the sheets washed, the kitchen and bathroom were clean, the kitchen was organized with clean plates, dishes and silverware and she had to make sure the apartment was comfortable and inviting.

Mom's Memorial Service was July 5. The whole family came in from LA and Las Vegas. Invitations were sent out, the band was booked and the church service was finalized. We selected beautiful readings and the immediate family participated.

Mary: We all arrived for Mom's service from all over the country. Ann, Chee and Paul selected the readings and Ann contacted the priest, Rev. Joseph Porpiglia, who was soon to be on vacation on his Harley in Colorado. We had to make sure he would be back on time. Our banker friends, Patrick and Joan Cullen, told us how beautifully the church was remodeled so we wanted to make sure we could have the service there. The family has great memories of this church. Saint Mary's Catholic Church was the church we went to in the summer when we stayed at the farm. Afterward, we'd go to the Drug Store and get candy. For Mom's service, friends and neighbors from Burke Parkway joined us along with the Cattaraugus friends. My son, Rick, did a reading form the book of Sirach 26:1-4, 13-16 and his two year old son, Evan, followed Rick up to the altar. Rick picked him up and read with Evan in his arms—grandson and great grandson saying goodbye to our inspirational matriarch.

Happy the husband of a good wife, twice-lengthened are his days;

A worthy wife brings joy to her husband,

Peaceful and full is his life.

A good wife is a generous gift,

Bestowed upon him who fears the Lord;

Be rich or poor, his heart is content,

And a smile is ever on his face.

A gracious wife delights her husband,

Her thoughtfulness puts flesh on his bones;

A gift from the Lord is her governed speech,

And her firm virtue is of surpassing worth.

Choicest of blessings is a modest wife,

Priceless her chaste person.

Like the sun rising in the Lord's heavens,

The beauty of a virtuous wife is the radiance of her home.

The word of the Lord.

It was so sweet. Our mom and dad loved each other their whole lives. Our dad built the home we grew up in and our mom decorated it with great taste and comfort. They were a wonderful team. It seemed to us that a lifetime wasn't long enough for them. That's why this reading was a perfect tribute for them both.

James Lullo, grandson from Chee, shared a reading from the second Letter of Saint Paul to Timothy 4:6-8.

Beloved:

I am already being poured out like a libation,

And the time of my departure is at hand.

I have completed well; I have finished the race;

I have kept the faith.

From now on the crown of righteousness awaits me,

Which the Lord, the just judge,

Will award to me on that day, and not only to me,

But to all who have longed for his appearance.

The word of the Lord.

Maribell Reid was 96 years old and she lived longer than all her friends and family so she won the race and was proud of it!

Gino sang so magnificently, Ave Maria and Our Father. Mom loved it. You could feel her presence. Ann read Psalm 23, "The Lord is my shepherd . . ." and wrote a beautiful original composition: Agnus Dei (Lamb of God) for Gino, flute (Jamie Newman) and organ (Mary Stoll).

Paul selected a reading from the Gospel and we discovered that Father Porpiglia had to read it. It's an unconventional reading for a funeral, but Paul was adamant that it was included. We all felt that our mom and dad were meeting in heaven to continue their lives together. The reading is from John, Chapter 2, The Wedding at Cana:

On the third day there was a wedding in Cana in Galilee, and the mother of Jesus was there.

Jesus and his disciples were also invited to the wedding.

When the wine ran short, the mother of Jesus said to him, "They have no wine."

And Jesus said to her, "Woman, how does your concern affect me? My hour has not yet come."

His mother said to the servers, "Do whatever he tells you."

Now there were six stone water jars there for Jewish ceremonial washings,

Each holding twenty to thirty gallons.

Jesus told them, "Fill the jars with water." So they filled them to the brim.

Then he told them, "Draw some out now and take it to the headwaiter." So they took it.

And when the headwaiter tasted the water that had become wine, without knowing

Where it came from (although the servers who had drawn the water knew,) the headwaiter called the bridegroom

And said to him, "Everyone serves good wine first, and then when people have drunk freely, the inferior one; but you have kept the good wine until now."

Jesus did this as the beginning of his signs in Cana in Galilee and so revealed his glory,

And his disciples began to believe in him.

The Gospel of John.

I did the eulogy. I talked about Mom flying down Waverly Street on the bobsled and putting the milk truck in neutral and soaring down Snyder Hill road on the way to People's Dairy in Blasdell. That's where I get my dare devil streak! I had to laugh. Our mom and dad met in high school in Blasdell. Mom was a senior and Dad was a junior. Dad told me it took him a year to ask her out. He was a big football and basketball star. Mom was witty, beautiful and alarming. No wonder our dad fell in love with her. She became a teacher in her late forties and started a new career with our dad's support. Retired teachers attended the service. We all had tears in our eyes as we said goodbye in our own way. We had a picnic at the farmhouse because that's what we always did in our family. Picnic! So everyone joined us at the farm. Mom loved Pete Fountain so Ann contacted musicians from SUNY Fredonia School of Music to play in the great room. We hired a clarinetist/ saxophonist (Dave Golondo), a guitarist (Tom Gestwicki) and a bassist (Harry Jacobson). They called themselves Dave Golondo & Friends and they were perfect. It was a warm, lazy summer day and we could sense Mom tapping her foot. She is now laid to rest near our dad. About thirty years ago they decided to be cremated and buried by the big pond. There were two trees with crooks in them and they sat in their perspective crooks in the tree and made big life decisions together. One of those decisions was to be buried together here near the pond where the deer like to rest and take refuge from the blistery winter storms. Chee's husband Mike made a beautiful wooden box for Mom's ashes. They are together now in the sanctuary we made for them. People thought Mom and Dad were movie stars when they were young. They reminded me of Clark Gable and Carol Lombard.

Maribell Scholl Reid

Richard Joseph Reid

There's a beautiful marble bird bath and marker stones. Ann bought and installed a wooden bridge so we can cross over the stream from the natural spring water which feeds into the pond. The sanctuary is a glorious place to think and be peaceful. In the summer, we can always swim over to the sanctuary or take the paddle boat and say a prayer, have a talk or just say hi. It's nice knowing they are both there together. Now we have to take care of the farm and make sure our children and grandchildren love it and care for it like we do. We have to be stewards of the land and our mom and dad are there overseeing us to make sure we do what's right.

Gino and Mary's Wedding

Chee: A couple more good parties at the farm; Paul's Burning Dog Festival was a big success the end of September. We met a cousin on Dad's side, Dad's cousin Gerry Reid Walker's son Kris and his wife came from Watkins Glen. (Gerry is Great-Uncle Max's daughter. Kris grew up in Varysburg and owns some hunting land there.)

Ann left for LA on November 1. She immediately went to Hawaii with her friends Susan and Jerry for their 50th wedding anniversary. Then everyone converged on the scene to enjoy Mary's wedding on November 23, 2013. Even Mike Lullo made it to LA. Gino and Mary were married at Saint Patrick's Italian Catholic Church in Los Angeles then caravanned to the Hotel Bel Air for the gorgeous reception. Another beautiful celebration!

Mary: My wedding to Gino was gorgeous, touching and personal. We were able to get married in the Catholic Church because neither one of us was married in the church previously. It was a little bit of an ordeal to get all the paperwork sorted out but it came together perfectly. I always say, "At the moment of commitment, the universe conspires to support you." I don't know where I heard this but I live by it. Father Raniero was funny and warm. I could hear people laughing before I walked down the aisle to meet my husband. Our grandchildren stole the show. My quartet played Bach's Air for my processional. All I can say is that it was magical. Our families and friends participated by sharing readings that Gino and I selected for the ceremony. Our friend Marcelo read this from Song of Solomon or Son of Songs 2:10-13:

My beloved speaks and says to me: Arise, my love, my fair one, and come away; for now the winter is past, the rain is over and gone. The flowers appear on the earth; the time of singing has come, and the voice of the turtledove is heard in our land. The fig tree puts forth its figs, and the vines are in blossom; they give forth fragrance. Arise, my love, my fair one, and come away.

We selected this because we both had horrible divorces and we were so grateful to find each other and start a new and wonderful life together. We raised our kids and they selected the best partners, husbands/wives and had kids of their own, so it was our turn to be happy! I think we're still in shock that it's working out so perfectly! How did we find each other? We can't believe it but we are so grateful. Chee and Mike shared A Reading From the First Letter of Saint Paul to the Corinthians 12:31-13:8A:

Brothers and Sisters:

Strive eagerly for the greatest spiritual gifts.

But I shall show you a still more excellent way.

If I speak in human and angelic tongues

But do not have love,

I am a resounding gong or a clashing cymbal.

And if I have the gift of prophecy

And comprehend all mysteries and all knowledge;

If I have all faith so as to move mountains,

But do not have love, I am nothing.

If I give away everything I own,

And If I hand my body over so that I may boast

But do not have love, I gain nothing.

Love is patient, love is kind.

It is not jealous, is not pompous,

It is not inflated, it is not rude,

It does not seek its own interests,

It is not quick-tempered, it does not brood over injury,

It does not rejoice over wrongdoing

But rejoices with the truth.

It bears all things, believes all things,

Hopes all things, endures all things.

Love never fails.

The word of the Lord.

We thought it would be appropriate for Chee and Mike to share this because they're still married after 25 plus years, not to mention the fact that they raised/are raising three wonderful kids—Jim, Joe and Mikey.

Father Raniero Alessandrini C. S. married us and was such a marvelous guide in this journey. He's Italian, of course, and Gino met him because he liked to go to the Italian mass at St. Peter's in Los Angeles on Broadway and listen. One day Father Raniero asked Gino if he would do a reading and Gino said, "Father I'm not Catholic." Father Raniero said, "That's ok, everyone's welcome in God's house." That's when Gino decided to convert. We selected a short, beautiful reading from the Gospel, According to John 15:9-12:

Jesus said to his disciples:

"As the Father loves me, so I also love you.

Remain in my love.

If you keep my commandments, you will remain in my love,

Just as I have kept my Father's commandments
And remain in his love.
I have told you this so that my joy might be in you
And your joy might be complete.
This is my commandment: love one another as I love you."
The Gospel of the Lord.

Ann walked down the aisle with Nina Gaudio, Gino's sister, and performed the Presentation of the Gifts.

Nina Gaudio and Ann Reid

The quartet played Largo by Handel for them. It was very sweet seeing our sisters together, especially knowing Ann almost didn't make it. I can't imagine her not being at the wedding, especially with mom gone. The reception was at the Hotel Bel Air on Stone Canyon Road in Bel Air, California.

Paul, Chee, me and Ann at Saint Peter's Italian
Catholic Church in Los Angeles.

Our kids: Marla & Rick Jacobs, Me and Gino, Bobby & Gratci Gaines,
Erick & Gemma Keldrauk. It was a dream come true reception.
Intimate like the wedding ceremony.

Now this is really interesting. Gino and I were on our honeymoon—June 2014 (we wanted to wait till it was warm to go to Italy) and I decided to buy a book for the plane. I chose *David and Goliath: Underdogs, Misfits, and the Art of Battling Giants* by Malcolm Gladwell because I had read *The Tipping Point* and *Outliers* so I knew the book would be interesting. I started the chapter on Emil "Jay" Freirich called "How Jay Did It, I Don't Know". Jay Freireich's family background was Hungarian. His family were immigrants who ran a restaurant in Chicago. The stock market crashed in 1929 and they lost everything, even Jay's father who committed suicide. Freireich's mother had to work so she got a job in a sweat shop and Jay and his sister never saw her. An Irish maid was hired and she was the only mother Freireich knew. When he was nine years old, his mother remarried but it was a miserable marriage of convenience. The maid was fired, they moved from apartment to apartment and Freireich was angry. He lived on the street and stole to get by. He came down with tonsillitis and the local physician, Dr. Rosenbloom, took care of him. In those days, everyone Freireich knew was a woman so he was very impressed seeing a man who was wearing a suit and tie, clean, dignified and kind. He began dreaming about becoming a doctor. His high school physics teacher encouraged him and his mother found the necessary money. Freireich graduated from the University of Illinois and began his internship at Cook County Hospital. He became a research associate in hematology in Boston, was drafted into the army and completed his military service at the National Cancer Institute, near Washington, DC. Gordon Zubrod was his boss and he assigned Freireich to the children's leukemia ward, which was the worst kind of cancer. A child would come down with a fever, followed by a severe headache, then infections and then bleeding. They bled internally, into their livers and spleens, and most of the time they died before anyone could figure out how to help. "Ninety percent of the kids would be dead in six weeks," said Freireich. Most doctors could not handle the leukemia ward. "Nobody wanted to work there. I had seventy kids who died on me that year. It was a nightmare."

Peter de Vries wrote a novel called *The Blood of the Lamb* sharing his experience over the death of his daughter. He wrote:

So we were back in the Children's Pavilion, and there was again the familiar scene: the mothers with their nearly dead, the false face of mercy, the Slaughter of the Innocents. A girl with one leg came unsteadily down the hall between crutches, skillfully encouraged by nurses. Through the pane in a closed door a boy could be seen sitting up in bed, bleeding from everything in his head; a priest lounged alertly against the wall, ready to move in closer. In the next room a boy of five was having Methotrexate pumped into his skull, or, more accurately, was watching a group of mechanics gathered solemnly around the stalled machine. In the next a baby was sitting up watching a television set on which a panel show was in progress . . . Among the parents and children, flung together in a hell of prolonged farewell, wandered forever the ministering vampires from Laboratory, sucking samples from bones and veins to see how went with each the enemy that had marked them all. And the doctors in their butchers' coats, who severed the limbs and gouged the brains and knifed the vitals where the demon variously dwelt, what did they think of these best fruits of ten million hours of dedicated toil? They hounded the culprit from organ to organ and joint to joint till nothing remained over which to practice their art: the art of prolonging sickness.

This was the look of leukemia at the time. Soon, another researcher named Tom Frei became a partner with Jay Freireich and they believed that there was a lack of platelets in the blood so it couldn't clot. All the doctors they worked with were skeptical but Freireich and Frei decided to recruit blood donors anyway. The equipment in the mid 1950s for blood transfusions wasn't working so Freireich used a new technology of silicon needles and plastic bags. The clinical director told him he was insane and that he was going to be fired if he continued the transfusions. Freireich didn't care and ignored his boss. He knew he was doing the right thing and "the bleeding stopped". This was a breakthrough! At least they could keep the children alive long enough to treat the illness. The drugs used were 6-MP, methotrexate, and a steroid called prednisone. Each drug was extremely toxic so small dosages were used. The children would get better for a week but then the leukemia would return. The leading doctor of hematology thought that the drugs would just prolong the death sentence of their patients.

Here is the interesting news! Freireich and Frei worked with a group in Buffalo, NY lead by James Holland at the Roswell Park Memorial Cancer Institute! Freireich and Frei were certain that those doctors had it all wrong! They believed that more drugs should be used, not less, to kill the cancer cells. Freireich also found another drug called vincristine which is derived from the periwinkle plant. He said he had twenty-five children who were dying and they had nothing to lose if he tried it on them. The drug had side effects and a couple children actually died. Freireich and Frei wanted to use four drugs at once but the board turned them down. "Anything more aggressive than that is unethical, and giving four drugs at a time is unconscionable." Zubrod, their boss, finally approved the use of vincristine. The process was called the VAMP regimen and children started living. They found they had to give several rounds of the treatment before the cancer stopped returning. In this process, "the children had to be brought savagely and repeatedly to the brink of death". The idea of combining the drugs came next and they were the first to come up with the drug "cocktails".

"Progress and Perspectives in the Chemotherapy of Acute Leukemia" was published by Freireich and Frie in 1965 in the journal *Advances in Chemotherapy* stating that they had "developed a successful treatment for childhood leukemia. Today the cure rate for this form of cancer is more than 90 percent". Did I tell you why this is important? This is the leukemia that Ann had—Acute Lymphocytic Leukemia, which was so unusual for an adult woman. Can you believe this? On top of this, Freireich came up with another cure. He took blood from patients who had chronic mycloid leukemia (CML), which overproduces white blood cells, and gave it to children with Acute Lymphocytic Leukemia (ALL). Freireich stated, "Everyone said it was insane. What if the children ended up somehow getting CML as well? What if it made them even sicker? This was an environment where the kids had one hundred percent mortality in months. We had nothing to lose." These men and this research saved Ann's life. We are so thankful that they had the courage and bravery to believe in what they were doing and not take "no" or "you're insane" for an answer.

Recovery

In October 2013, Ann was referred to City of Hope in Los Angeles by her Roswell doctors. She also started going to weSPARK which is a support group in Sherman Oaks, CA for people with cancer. It was started by a friend of Tom Hanks and Stephen Spielberg, Wendy Jo Sperber. Her goal was to create a cancer support center with a home-like setting to enhance the lives of cancer patients and their families. weSPARK opened in 2001 and families continue to be helped through their ordeals. She lost her battle to cancer but she left behind an incredible safe haven for people of all ages to share their fears and hopes for survival. Ann needed to find her way this winter and she has a long way to go still. The doctors were trying to stabilize her because she had the Graft vs. Host disease and she was on a high dosage of steroids. Because of the steroids she had to deal with diabetes. weSPARK was able to help her with a nutritionist so she could get her diet under control and she discovered that sugar was the worst thing for her. She also had neuropathy in her feet from all the chemo treatments. At weSPARK they offered Tai Chi and foot massages which helped her tremendously. She was falling constantly and gave us some good scares when she was all bruised and battered. Her skin was so thin it almost peeled off when she got hurt. Her skin is still this way and the neuropathy has not gone away. The doctors say that it's the steroids that are making her skin thin and her face puffy. The steroids control the Graft vs. Host disease so this is a delicate balance to get the right combination and of course she is constantly changing.

When she got all set with her medical transfer, I took Ann to City of Hope in her Smart Car, and she told me, "The doctors wanted me to have a colonoscopy because I was having some issues with Graft vs. Host disease. Well, I said no because I'm scared to death. This is what happened to me. I had one in 2009 and my colon burst because of the medication you take the day before. Everyone was freaking out and I was in an induced coma. The doctor at City of Hope said he'd never seen that in thirty years of practicing. I told him I could get the hospital information for him, "No, no", he said. Remember we all thought that it lead to the leukemia because of the infection, my body couldn't fight it anymore. We were at mom's house in Blasdell and she called 911 and she gave her address and everything. Then she called Antonio, our neighbor. I was really surprised. She was about 90 and at the beginning of her dementia. I'm lying there screaming! It was really painful, more painful than childbirth even. We called the ambulance and I passed out completely. I thought . . . I told Chee, "They gave me this good medication to knock me out" and Chee said that I passed out and I never woke up again for two weeks. They had me in an induced coma. Evidently, they called Chee, and said you better get here, your sister's vital signs are going down. "What?" Chee didn't even know that I was there, in the hospital. So Chee went to the hospital thinking they were going to tell her I'm going to be alright, but they were telling her that her sister is "going". Chee had to take over and she started making sure that people were taking care of me. She said, "Why aren't the doctors here? She's been lying there for hours and nobody has come to see her." They didn't know that I was getting peritonitis. It must have been a mess! Then they finally recognized that there was something going wrong. They got me in an operation and they discovered what was going on. They took out fourteen inches of my colon, cleaned me out and put me in an induced coma. So the funny thing is, I know you were there, but I don't know if you remember. I was still in the hospital but I was ok. So Paul says to me, "So what good hallucinations did you have?" I never thought of it, but he made me think, well I was on a trip around the world! And everything was yellow; a Turkish man showed me how to make pizza; I was on the gold yacht in the Arabian Gulf, and I was with this Arabian family and they wanted me to take their son to LA to teach him the music business. And then I had this hallucination that I was in LA and I'm trying to rent my condo. So I had this telephone call, this is all hallucination, I'm so upset, I have to return this call, so I get the attendant to tell me, he was a guy, and I said, "I've got to call my office, I've got to call my office . . . I got a call about my condo". By that time my office was on this boat in Alaska and we were fishing in Alaska! I kept telling him, I've gotta call, I've gotta call. "Ok, I'll get the phone", he said. I'm awake enough that I hear them all laughing, and I did wake up after that. When I woke up I thought you had put on this gorgeous yellow outfit just for me and you were all radiant with the sunshine around you. I never saw anything so pretty. And it was your sterilization gown!!! Everybody had to wear them but I never saw anyone else with it on, just you. Everyone was thinking, oh poor Ann and the whole family is going crazy, they called my son and told him your mom is the hospital and she may die. And Ann is on a trip around the world!

So after the Bone Marrow Transplant, I was learning how to play the ukulele. Someone told them I was a musician. When I was in the hospital for leukemia, I set myself all up with my music, my CDs and my music boom box. I was listening to contemporary orchestral music and things like that. I also had my synthesizer there, or my keyboard which just transmits to the computer for writing. I've got my computer there all the time and I'm writing my music and I was also teaching my online course—History of Rock and Roll. This was my first hospital stay for leukemia. I was admitted to the hospital four times I think. The first was for leukemia from February till July. I got out in July for the big party at the farm. I had to stay so long because I had an infection that wouldn't heal. The doctor knew Dr. Rosen at Case Western who put me back together after the colonoscopy disaster. I had to wear a bag for almost a year. They had to reattach the colon and sew me up. One doctor attached the colon and the other doctor sewed me up but every time they sewed me I would rip open again. So they had to put in the mesh and everything was fine. Then when I had the leukemia, one of the reasons I was going to the clinic was that I had an infection in my back that wouldn't heal. It just kept opening up so I went to the clinic in Batavia and they kept giving me antibiotics but it wasn't healing. So I finally went to the doctor and she took three different blood tests because she started suspecting. By the third blood test she called me on Saturday morning and told me you have to go to the hospital. She didn't say why

*and I thought oh no I'm just tired. I want to go home and go to bed. I
don't know why I called Chee, but I did and told her, well, the doctor said
I should go to the hospital but I'm just tired so I'm going to go home and
go to bed. And Chee said Oh no, and she came and got me and we went
to Mercy, good thing. Mercy Hospital took blood tests and put me in an
ambulance to Roswell right away. So when I got to Roswell, I'm lying in bed
there, nobody told me yet what it was. At first they said, what's that disease
everybody gets in college? Mononucleosis. They discover that it wasn't the
mesh that got infected, it was the staples which tore a hole in the mesh and
caused the infection. They took the staples out and I was in the hospital a
couple weeks more and I went to the rehab home. The nurses came to see
me every day and swabbed out the infection and redressed it. I gradually
healed. They let me out of the rehab to go to the July party. I was so anxious
to go to the party. I wanted to be free by July. I went in again five days
before the Bone Marrow Transplant, so I went into the hospital on October
19th with five more days of chemo. They have to kill everything, so that
the bone marrow is completely dead. My hair fell out from the leukemia
but it fell out a second time. That was interesting because the first time, I
have a picture of me playing the piano and Gino was singing, and I have
little shreds of straight hair. When it came in after the bone marrow, it was
curly. After the transplant, the head of a dance company from NYC came
into my room. (I want to send him my script and ask him if it could be
a ballet. I would love it to be a ballet. I could see all the ideas that I have
in my head.) The doctors and nurses told him I was a musician. So I said,
here's something, do you want to hear this? So I put it through my speakers
so he could hear it real well and he liked it! I told him the whole story and
he came back a few days later with his two lead dancers—a guy and a girl.
The guy liked the Muslim part where Aelinor was abducted and taken back
to the harem. I had the overture on my computer and played it for him.
They did a whole dance for me in my room dancing to my music. They
came right to my room! That was part of this UB (University at Buffalo)
program where evidently they got a twenty million dollar grant for art in
the hospital. They not only went to Roswell but they were going to children's
hospitals and many other places. They brought art classes more than once
a week. We would design post cards; I made a little bird; and we did all
these little art projects. I made an Obama mask, too. I have to say, art and*

laughter, we laughed so much. There was the art person and then there was another person who was a set designer. We created the mask with strips of newspaper, paper mache. We laughed and laughed, the nose had to be just so and the ears had to stick out. We couldn't decide what color—if you see him on TV he just looks sun tanned. I got such a kick out of it. The next day was Election Day so I put the mask on and told everybody to vote for me. That was great fun. Oh yes, I put the mask on as soon as I woke up, very early, maybe 5:00 or 5:30 AM. The nurse didn't come till around 6:00. I laid in bed and when the nurse arrived, she screamed and ran to get her supervisor. They came in and they looked at me and they realized it was a mask. She told me there is actually a complication where the ears get big! She thought I had this bad combination of drugs! I thought it was so funny that she didn't recognize that it was a mask. Oh I have to tell you, I had just enough hair at that time and it was exactly like Obama's hair! It was short and curly, dark and straight across.

Back to the Bone Marrow Transplant, I had to be tested three times and that was very painful. The BMT itself is just the stem cells. You just lay there and it's like a blood donation, except it takes a long time. I asked the doctor, how do they know they are bone marrow cells? He said, "Each one has a little mark, each cell, they have their own mark, and they knew they were stem cells. I had the idea, it wasn't a hallucination, but all the little stem cells, they were marching into the bone marrow singing "I'm a bone marrow, I'm a bone marrow, I'm a bone marrow, too!" You know, I said to the doctor, "How do they know they aren't a nose or an eye because they're undifferentiated, except for the little marker and they knew they were bone marrow". So it came to me, this vision of them marching into my bones. It probably helped me recover!

Mary: So far we think that Ann will be at the farm part time and in Batavia near Chee. Then she'll spend the winter in Los Angeles. She was getting the kitchen gardens ready for planting at the farm last summer so she could grow her organic vegetables. In Batavia, she was organizing her home after all the chaos subsided. Because of the Graft vs. Host disease, they may have to cleanse her blood with infra red and see if that will take care of it. But they are holding off on that for now.

I'm not as scared anymore when the phone rings. We can just say hi and catch up with each other. Chee's son James is out in Los Angeles now and trying his hand in acting. Her other son, Joe, is here visiting before he finishes his Bachelor of Science degree in Biology at the University at Buffalo. Ann still has strange reactions to some of her medications. She wants to be off the steroids at least but now a reaction is that she is very weak. She also had problems with pain in her legs. We're coming up on her two year birthday of her Bone Marrow Transplant. It may take a couple more years for her to stabilize. Probably the hardest thing for her is to be patient. It's probably the hardest for all of us. We don't know what it's like on this side of the transplant for anyone. Will she have to take steroids for the rest of her life? I know she wants to stabilize herself and not have to go to doctors so often. She was going to go to London with Jack but that's not possible now. She had to go back to the "Roswell Spa" because she fell and we were concerned about her balance. We found out she had an infection in her leg. They put her on an IV drip with antibiotics. Travel plans were up in the air but she finally stabilized and Joe flew with her when she came back to Los Angeles. We don't want her living alone anymore so she'll be staying with her son and daughter-in-law for the time being.

There are several different endings to this story. Now the question is: Will Ann live happily ever after at Beauty View Farm, making and marketing her apple wine? Will she live happily ever after with her son and daughter-in-law in sunny southern LA? Will she live happily ever after doing a show on Broadway living in NYC? Will she live happily ever after traveling the world to her time shares? Or is it a mixture of all of these scenarios: maybe she'll be in Italy and rent a bunch of rooms/houses. Whoever can and wants to go visit her will join Ann near Trevinnano, Italy and we'll drink wine, make pasta, hike, swim and have fun the Italian way.

By the way, I didn't know what I wanted to name the book. I asked for Chee's, Paul's and Ann's opinion because I wanted everyone to be happy with the outcome. It started out "Ann's Life" as a working title and moved to "Ann's Leukemia". Then Chee suggested "Happily Ever

After . . ." and it morphed into "Happily Ever . . ." because we didn't
know what that looks like at all. Then I tried "Tarzan, Funny Girl, Hair
and Leukemia" because she was in the three shows and that turned
into "Hair and Leukemia". Chee thought of "The Three Sisters" which
seemed like a modern day Chekhov play to me.

We don't know where this is going or what's going to happen still.
Every day is a new experience and we just keep moving through the
air. What will happen next? What is this new concept? What is the
new normal? Shift and change is the new way. Who will Ann spend
her life with? Will she get better or is this as good as it gets? There are
so many questions. Ann is adamant that she will be well which is very
good. I like to hear that positive intention. But we don't know what
reality is at this time. We think all is fine and she has a huge set-back.
Ten steps forward and five steps back. We thought she'd respond to the
new DNA with no problems not knowing about the Graft vs. Host
disease. She gets the rash on her back, arms, legs, in her mouth and in
her stomach. She has to take steroids to stop the itch. Now she is trying
steroid cream and an antihistamine. She keeps getting infections, too,
and we don't know why. The infection in her leg was simply crazy
and the doctors couldn't figure it out at first either. She is very wobbly
still and Ann says it's from the medications that she has to take. It's
throwing us for a bit of a loop. I keep thinking that she has to live
now. It's time to take the precious articles and remembrances out of
the hope chest and use them, this is it. No more hoping, it's time for
living. Make decisions and get rid of things that encumber you so you
are free to move around. If you are declared cancer free in three more
years, then you'll have all decisions made and you won't be in limbo
for three years waiting for life to begin. Or if things don't go well, your
son and your sisters won't be obligated to go through your things and
make decisions for you! But I'm just the little sister. What do I know?

After living through closing our mom's house and looking through all
her possessions and seeing what Ann is going through, I'm starting to
organize my things and eliminate/discard things I don't love. I look in
the stores and wonder where this will all go if it's not sold. What storage

facility will hold it? What country will give it to their people? Where do all the chatskis go? There's too much stuff in this world! If aliens landed, what would they think and say to us? Don't get me wrong, I'm still a consumer but I think about it. Do I really need that purse even though I want it? I try to buy one good thing that I love rather than lots of little cheap things. I took 10 bags of stuff to Goodwill over Thanksgiving break! For Ann's Christmas present, I bought her a chest of drawers and Gino and I went to her house in Van Nuys and organized her bedroom. She is still discombobulated and can't make decisions where things should be located. You have to take everything out of the chair if you want some place to sit down in her room. Anything she doesn't wear regularly was tossed. If it was ugly, out it went! This will be practice for the house in Batavia. If she's going to sell it, lots of decisions need to be made—Keep, Give Away, Sell, Throw Out!

We all know it's not easy but you have to start. Just begin and push through the anguish. Start out doing a little bit every day. There's a book about a ten minute a day dissertation. Basically, if you just sit at your computer everyday and do something, you end up staying longer and more gets done than you expected. That's what happened to me with my dissertation. If you can discipline yourself to put on your seat belt at your computer every day, you will accomplish something! I started writing around 7:00 PM after work and before I knew it, it was 2:00 AM. It's difficult! I get it! Procrastination? Just stop it! Boredom? Just stop it! Lazy? Just stop it! Confused? Just stop it! Start! Start something! Anything! No more excuses, even though they may be good ones. Continue doing whatever it is you love until you can't.

So I asked Ann, "How do you see the world now? How do you fit in this world now?"

And she told me, "Where am I now, over two years after my initial diagnosis—leukemia and then the bone marrow transplant? Well, whenever I complain to my doctors they only remind me, "you are alive!"

Now I remember, looking back, exactly what happened when I was told I actually had leukemia. The medical team was standing around my bed at Roswell. Dr. Elizabeth Griffiths said, "You have leukemia. If you hadn't come in today you would have been dead in two weeks." I heard the information but I was numb. Dr. Griffiths said, "You have Acute Lymphoblastic Leukemia and it's very fast moving." As she was talking the nurses were hooking me up to the chemo. She said, "We have been working on this for twenty five years and our treatment is highly successful." My thoughts went to, this is a Sunday and I was stunned that anyone was even there to start the treatment so immediately. I didn't have time to assimilate the information and I was already being treated. It was like an opera, Dr. Griffiths was the soloist and there were a whole cast of characters who were taking care of me. She saved my life.

Yes, that is very wonderful. I frequently wonder how I can possibly still be alive. I am in "recovery". How long? Who knows? Doctors say that if I am still alive after four years, I am cured. But I am always worried. What next? I am feeling better and better and that is good, but is some gremlin following me about ready to strike again? I am still pretty private, remaining at home or attending theatre or the opera and symphony without any fanfare. I am sort of hiding from everyone, except for my dearly beloveds. I feel that my illness has played a cruel trick on my face and body. Three years ago I was a professor of music and taught many courses and was in charge of music for the musical. I had long, blonde hair and lots of energy. Now, there is the new reality. I am tired. I wobble and have to walk with a cane and take a walker for long distances. I am covered with wrinkles and my bits of hair are grey and thin.

But that is all cosmetic. I am alive. I live in Los Angeles for the winter and Western New York for the summer. I visit friends and go out to lunch. I am slowly selling everything I bought for my "old age". I think my old age has begun. I can't eat sugar or drink wine. But is that bad? I eat green soup and shop at hideously expensive organic food stores. I am trying to grow the necessary greens organically in my own farm garden. That is a project I look forward to.

I am intent on getting my work, "AElinor, the Oratorio", performed by a professional company, orchestra, or ballet. I am working on my mini-musical, "Bluebird" about the New York State bird, now in jeopardy of becoming extinct. "Leukemia, the Musical" is now in the planning stages. Other works for string quartet, orchestra, chorus, and children are in the works. i.e. my head.

If you have been told you need chemo, steroids and bone marrow transplant, do it. My comments above pertain to me and my search for the new me. Much, much work has been done on the treatments for leukemia. Doctors have over twenty five years of study and findings to make your recovery as fast and comfortable as possible. They are all interested in "success", too. I was sent to Roswell Park Cancer Institute upon my diagnosis. The work of the doctors, nurses, Fellows and assistants is outstanding. I was actually pretty happy there and felt that the doctors were sincerely interested in me and my recovery. We got through many incidences where they had to search above and beyond normal recovery (the "meow, meow" issue written in the book above is one of them).

I had to have care 24/7 for 100 days after my release from hospital for the bone marrow transplant. The hospital Social Services suggested Hope Lodge, an old mansion on Delaware Avenue, renovated and taken over by the American Cancer Society. I was allowed to spend the entire 100 days there FOR FREE! Besides the fact I was still pretty much in bed, I enjoyed the family members and friends who came to take care of me for a week or two at a time. They actually had fun living in the huge old house, making meals (especially the Philippine cooking by my daughter-in-law) sorting out the interminable pills I had to take and socializing with the other bone marrow transplant people staying there.

Doctors told me that I should not live alone. I decided to go out to LA and have my son and daughter-in-law look after me. Doctors at Roswell recommended City of Hope. I transferred there and bought a little Smart Car to get out there for appointments. I started my regime of appointments with the doctors at City of Hope. That went very well and I progressed to feeling very well.

My wellness had a lot to do with weSPARK, a cancer support group on Ventura Boulevard in Sherman Oaks, CA. EVERYTHING there was FREE! I Took Tai Chi, hypnosis, reflexology, support group and everything else I could get down there for. My experience there was outstanding. I miss the weSPARK staff very much and hope to continue my classes when I get back in the winter.

Now, I will get back with the doctors at Roswell Park. They will follow my progress until next winter. I am anxious to get off all the pills I am taking. Doctors still feel they are necessary but they also add to my wobbliness and other side effects. It will be great when I am taking NO medications. That is a goal.

Other goals have to do with me getting stronger and stronger, walking farther and farther, writing and writing more music, shows and orchestral works.

I would like to thank all of the doctors that helped me survive. I sent an email to Dr. Elizabeth Griffiths and here is the following correspondence:

Hi Dr. Griffiths!

Would you send me a list of the chemo drugs you used for my leukemia treatment when diagnosed in February 2012? My sister is writing a book about sisters and how they coped with another sister with leukemia.

Also, I am a singer and when I got severe laryngitis you were so worried that you had taken away my voice. Who is the doctor that discovered large doses of Vitamin B6 for the condition?

My voice is back but is an octave lower.
We will send you a pdf of the book when finished.
Thank you for your attention to this detail.

Ann Reid

Dear Ann,

How lovely to hear from you. Happy Christmas and New Year!

The chemotherapy drugs you got included the following:

2 courses of induction including daunorubicin, vincristine and dexamethasone.

One course of consolidation including cyclophosphamide, doxorubicin dexamethasone and vincristine.

The vincristine was the drug we thought had caused your neuropathy (as well as your laryngitis).

Dr. Arshad was the ENT doctor who saw you in the hospital and suggested that perhaps high dose B-vitamins might make things better.

I'm so very pleased to hear that you recovered your voice!

I would love to read your sister's book.

Please let me know if you need any additional details about the chemotherapy you received.

Take good care of yourself!

Elizabeth Griffiths

Roswell Park Doctors:

Dr. Elizabeth Griffiths—leukemia

Dr. George Chen—BMT(Bone Marrow Transplant), Graft vs. Host Disease

Dr. Philip McCarthy—Director, BMT Center

Dr. Maureen Ross—BMT

Dr. Hong Liu—BMT

City of Hope:

Dr. Royotaro Nakamura – BMT

The main chemo drug that was used on me was vincristine. This drug belongs to a class of chemotherapy which is made from plants. The vinca alkaloids are made from the periwinkle plant (catharanthus roseus) and are cell specific. This means that they only affect the cells when they are dividing.

All the doctors will all appear in LEUKEMIA, THE MUSICAL, my next project! I have had some of the songs from AElinor recorded and two songs from Bluebird. That is a start. My nephew wants me to put some of my works in the "cloud". I want to get to know all the digital resources at my disposal. No going backwards, only forwards."

With gratitude and respect,

Ann

CPSIA information can be obtained at www.ICGtesting.com
Printed in the USA
BVOW08s1020130715

408543BV00003B/44/P